LANDMARK COLLECTOR'S LIBRARY

PAST TIMES
OF
MACCLESFIELD
VOLUME II

Dorothy Bentley Smith

Published by

Landmark Publishing Ltd
Ashbourne Hall, Cokayne Ave, Ashbourne, Derbyshire DE6 1EJ England
Tel: (01335) 347349 Fax: (01335) 347303
e-mail: landmark@clara.net
website: www.landmarkpublishing.co.uk

ISBN 1 84306 168 6

© **Dorothy Bentley Smith 2005**

British Library Cataloguing in Publication Data: a catalogue
record for this book is available from the British Library.

Print: Cromwell Press Ltd, Trowbridge
Design: Mark Titterton
Cover: James Allsopp

Front cover top left: The tomb effigy of Eleanor of Castile, reproduced by Courtesy of the Dean and Chapter
of Westminster; **Top right:** The present Gawsworth Hall; **Bottom left:** 18th century Macclesfield silk buttons
as produced by the Brocklehurst family; **Bottom right:** The school building of 1748-1910
on King Edward Street. **Title page:** Gate of Remembrance, The King's School.

LANDMARK COLLECTOR'S LIBRARY

PAST TIMES
OF
MACCLESFIELD

VOLUME II

Dorothy Bentley Smith

Landmark Publishing

Dedication

To my grand-daughters Megan Eveline and Charlotte Elizabeth
and all future generations.

'Ignorance is the first requisite of the historian-
ignorance, which simplifies and clarifies,
which selects and omits, with a placid perfection
unattainable by the highest art.'

Lytton Strachey (1880-1932)

Contents

Acknowledgements

Late in the summer of 1994 Granville Sellars, the then owner of the Macclesfield Community News, offered me the opportunity to write a series of local history articles for the free monthly newspaper. I eagerly accepted, but neither he nor I could have envisaged that ten years on I would still be contributing my column; and so to him must go my first vote of thanks.

It has been a fascinating and rewarding journey made possible, not only by the Macclesfield people of the past, but also those of the present who have helped in several ways. Many have generously given permission for property deeds to be examined; produced old books, long since removed from accessible bookshelves; donated photographs and information, and invited me into their homes.

I am also indebted to numerous solicitors; estate agents; personnel within banks, breweries, head offices of businesses investing in High Street shops; the Macclesfield Borough Council and the Silk Heritage Centre, for their co-operation. Nor must I forget the staff of the Cheshire County Record Office and Macclesfield Public Library who have been indefatigable in searching out relevant sources of information; and the Leeds District Archivist who spent time and effort in putting at my disposal a considerable volume of information from the large Radcliffe family archive (Pickford family) part of which was uncatalogued. Also to my eldest daughter, Victoria, whose skills and knowledge in the mysterious world of computers is second to none, and to the staff of Mailboxes Etc. who have given considerable assistance with illustrations over the years in reproducing specific details from photos and plans.

Last, but by no means least, my thanks must go to the excellent 'team' in the Community News offices, and in particular to the editor, Jean Ellis, whose support and encouragement over the last decade have been very much appreciated.

Foreword

To commemorate ten years of writing for the Macclesfield Community News, and with encouragement from my publisher and others, I decided that the time was right to produce a collection of my local history articles in book form.

Volume I covers articles written from the autumn of 1994 to August 1999, and volume II completes the series to date.

It is inevitable, when writing for a newspaper, that occasions will arise when editing takes place, or photographs and even articles omitted, because of limited space (for this reason no articles appeared in the September 2000 and 2001 editions). This has given me the opportunity to publish the unedited versions, correct errors where necessary and add the additional illustrations. I sincerely hope that both books will not only be of interest as a general read, but will also be used for research purposes and encourage a further generation to appreciate the wealth of history which lies within the borough of Macclesfield.

Dorothy Bentley Smith

Pott Croft – Exchange Street

Time after time my researches have produced some intriguing questions and it is always satisfying to find what appears to be a logical or correct answer.

Some time ago some interesting information was revealed in deeds relating to Derby Street, the street which originally ran from Chestergate south along Churchill Way, but then curved west midway between Castle Street and Exchange Street. A remnant of this street still remains behind the Tesco store on Exchange Street and is now known as Exchange Close.

The deeds appeared to relate to what is today part of the Marks & Spencer plc. site, and in one of the properties lived a spinster, Mary Watson who, by her will dated 16th February 1770, left several bequests

The entrance to Exchange Close between Tesco and W.H.Smith. In the centre background is the loading area for Marks & Spencer, formerly Pott Croft.

to various relatives, including her property. What makes her will unique is her initial 'demand' regarding burial; her desire – 'to be buried in my burying place and it may not be used for the internment of any other corpse for 50 years'!

This is an incredible request particularly given the circumstances regarding burials at that time. The Christ Church burial ground was, as yet, unavailable so the only place to 'go' was in the burial ground surrounding St. Michael's Church in the Market Place.

In 1775 the minister Rev. Thomas Hewson wrote to the Bishop of Chester advising him.'I can afsure your L'dship that it is now very difficult to find any place in the Chapel Yard where a Corpse can be buried. I have known it very lately, that two Coffins have been oblig'd to be taken up. & carried into the Chapel and remain there while another has been buried, & the People Dispers'd. & then the others bro't back into the same Grave, so that there has not, when cover'd, been a foot Depth of Soil upon them – I, as well as other Gentlemen in Macclesfield, have seen a Scull wch has been taken up, but cou'd not be avoided , & thrown

into a place where the Bones usually taken up in making Graves are put, wth the Flesh upon it in a corrupted State; wch is certainly Disagreeable to any person induced wth the least Spark of Humanity, & may, in all Probability, be the Cause of some Pestilential Disorder amongst us.'

We can now well understand Mary Watson's concern and hope that she did 'rest in peace'.

Along with several others her cottage or house adjoined 'a certain place . . . called Pott Croft' which allowed the local residents specific rights. One was to keep swine or asses upon the 'Common Midding Stead' in the croft and also the 'Liberty & privilege of going to & returning from & using the Common Privy House or House of Ease in Pott Croft . . . from time to time as need or occasion shall require'.

Pott Croft was obviously a fairly large area and although the deeds related to houses numbered 6-10 Derby Street (one of which must have belonged to Mary but in her day was not numbered) and two Courts 4 and 5, it was still a problem imagining where approximately the croft had been, but another source unexpectedly supplied the answer.

Thanks to the co-operation of Marks &

Spencer plc., and despite the fact that the deeds for the store at 33 Mill Street, Macclesfield are mostly post war, and therefore contain little of historical interest, yet there was sufficient information regarding several properties in the original Derby Street area to make the search worthwhile, for included in the batch were those for 6-10 Derby Street but only abstracted from 1902.

However the important item was a reference to a group of warehouses and buildings in Court 1, referred to as 'formerly Pott Croft'. And even more relevant was a plan clearly indicating that the most westerly part of the loading bay to the Marks & Spencer store – at the rear of the premises 33 Mill Street but situated between the store's rear entrance to Exchange Close and that part of the W.H. Smith building which extends into Exchange Street from Mill Street – was part of the original Pott Croft of the 18th century.

To date I have discovered two further middingsteads in the centre of the town, in what would have been the earlier borough; one in Dog Lane, which is now buried somewhere under the stalls in the middle of the Indoor Market; the other on the site of the Mothercare store at 30 Mill Street which, by a strange quirk

of fate, was previously the Marks & Spencer store before the company moved across to the opposite side of Mill Street in the late 1960s.

The two middingsteads on the west side of Mill St. (see plan of 1814 vol I pages 122-123) had probably existed for centuries, but the one on the Mothercare site was possibly from about the 16th century, because previously this had been the location of John of Macclesfield's residence often referred to as a castle.

Mention of the latter has provided me with the opportunity to write a few words regarding the controversy surrounding the correct title for the mansion. After the Norman Conquest of 1066 the word 'castle' entered the English language from the French which indicated a large building or set of buildings fortified for defence. It was also used (and still is) for things resembling a castle i.e. sand castle, but the main significance seems to be the fortification of the building. As John of Macclesfield not only obtained permission to 'kerneller' (crenellate) BUT also 'batailler' (embattle or protect for battle) is it so wrong for those in the past to have referred to it as a castle? It certainly doesn't warrant their condemnation.

Perhaps we should have a new title for the new millennium 'Macclesfield's Minicastle'!

Indoor Market 8th May 1995 : 50th anniversary V.E. Day celebrations: in this area in earlier centuries there was a middingstead with all its 'conveniences'.

Silk

Having returned from a fascinating trip to China in the autumn of 1999, it seemed appropriate to link it to Macclesfield's historic past.

Apart from standing on the Great Wall, the highlight of the visit was a civic welcome to the city of Xi'an, the ancient capital before the court was moved to Beijing. The city was of particular importance during the Tang Dynasty (618-907 A.D.) when masses of superb pottery figures and animals were produced using vibrant colours and glazes which were copied about 1,000 years later by the potters of Staffordshire.

(Incidentally it is recorded that Jesuit priests brought the ingredients and methods of porcelain manufacture to the West in the 16th century and as we shall see it was missionaries who had also brought the secrets of silk production in the same direction, but much earlier).

Xi'an was the last station on the silk road where provisions and goods were bought before some of the traders departed for Loyang; today in one of the old quarters a factory produces silk scarves and silk carpets, although the silk itself now comes from southern China.

On the outskirts of the city, of course, the terracotta army is beginning to tell its own intriguing stories, attracting visitors from all over the world.

Tired, thirsty and extremely hot after a long journey and walking beneath the ramparts of the ancient walls, by which our group was totally dwarfed (just as the traders for centuries must have experienced), the feeling was also one of awe and curiosity. All at once the massive red city gates came into view sporting their nine Imperial rows of huge brass studs, but barring the way was a contingent of 'Imperial guards'. Wondering what would happen next we were stopped in our tracks by a barrage of orders bellowed out in Chinese by the soldiers, and suddenly the enormous gates began to open accompanied by the sound of beating drums and wind instruments.

This was the ancient ceremony for welcoming 'guests' (i.e. prospective purchasers) re-enacted with costumes created as authentically as possible. The presentation was truly impressive, complete with a very long red carpet and dancers with silken banners.

'Government officials' swept towards us followed by a party of lovely girls dressed in beautiful richly coloured silk garments. We were each given a much welcomed cup of wine and a large 'antique' passport covered in silk (which on entering the courtyard through the gates was officially stamped by the 'Emperor's Emissary') and finally a replica gold key of the city on a knotted yellow cord, which was placed around the neck of each of the party.

For me this was so significant, for I immediately sensed that this was where Macclesfield's fame as a silk town had originally begun.

The earliest reference to silk is in the year

A figure representing John Lombe on a building in the centre of Derby. He is credited with setting up the first silk spinning mill in England using specialised machinery, the drawings and model of which he had smuggled out of Italy. Charles Roe also used this type of machinery when he later built the first large Macclesfield silk spinning mill.

An ancient ceremony welcoming guests into the city of Xi'an, the ancient capital of China and last station on the Silk Road.

2,640 B.C. when a Chinese Empress, Hsi Ling Shi was said to have devoted herself to the industry. Despite the desire of other nations to learn the secrets of the lucrative trade, China managed to maintain her monopoly for around 3,000 years.

Many myths and legends exist to support its eventual proliferation throughout the Far East and then into the West, but the basic facts are as follows:

About the third century, during periods of internal strife in northern China, refugees fleeing over the border into Korea took their industry with them, from where it spread into Japan. It was also thought to have been taken to India by a princess who, on marrying an Indian prince, had concealed some silkworm eggs in her elaborate headdress.

It supposedly came West through the activities of two monks in the 6th century A.D. who also smuggled some eggs out of China, but this time in a hollow cane, for which they were duly rewarded by the Emperor Justinian in Constantinople.

The Arabs soon acquired the techniques of production, carrying them to Spain, and as the Spanish extended their possessions in Italy, there too the industry became firmly established.

The earliest mention of a silk spinning mill in England was that built by a lawyer, Thomas Cotchet, in 1702 on one of the islands in the River Derwent close by the centre of Derby. The next stage of the story has several versions but all agree that Sir Thomas Lombe, a freeman of the City of London (and from 1727 member of the Mercers Company), assisted his half brother John on a mission of 'industrial espionage' to Piedmont in Italy, where the death penalty existed for just such a crime.

John (a possible former apprentice of Cotchet's mill) was successful and returned with Italian workmen to Derby where, in 1717, he began his grand scheme resulting in a magnificent large mill which became a tourist attraction. Sir Thomas soon took out a patent for the specialised machinery, which expired in 1732.

Almost immediately, on 24th June 1732, a group of six partners began construction of a silk mill complex in Stockport, and when an already existing building was adapted and included in the scheme on 1st May 1740, the premises were then completed.

There is no doubt that Charles Roe of Macclesfield would have visited the Derby mill and also had first hand knowledge of the Stockport enterprise when he made his decision to build a silk mill complex (also for spinning) in Macclesfield. The work began in the summer of 1743, and apart from a small Jacobite disruption when Bonnie Prince Charlie passed through the town in December 1745, was completed in 1748.

Amazingly because of the dedication and investment by local families and their associates, the Macclesfield silk industry became supreme and world famous, particularly during the 19th century and early years of the 20th century, despite occasional competition with cotton.

It had taken thousands of years and travelled thousands of miles to reach Macclesfield – a journey which I had completed in less than a day!

Misconceptions – Robert Roe's house and John de Macclesfield

This article was the opportunity to draw attention to some misconceptions which had come to light during my researches.

The first relates to the property originally 67 Roe Street but now 65A and 67 Roe Street which was the subject of the article on pages 128-131 (vol I), proving that Robert Roe's house was on Chestergate and not the above property. I was subsequently informed by a former resident of 65A that there was; a Wesley connection, also the architecture and fittings dated it around 1775, and that 63 and 65 were built 'considerably later' than 67, therefore he still considered it to have been Robert Roe's house.

The following additional information should dispel further argument.

Originally the Pickford family leased this area of parkland (today on the south side of Roe Street) from the Cholmondeley estate, and Charles Roe subleased from Pickford, because he needed control of the Dams Brook from his own land down to the silk mill complex on Parsonage (Park) Green. In 1770 Charles Roe leased directly from the Cholmondeleys and it is entered on the rental as 'part of Pickford's'. There were no buildings shown on this portion of the Roe St. land when the survey of 1778 was made not long before the great sale; the rental continued after Charles Roe's death in 1781, so it was son William who eventually bought that particular area.

The title deeds for 67 Roe Street show initially William Roe as owner of three properties in 1810, viz; 63, 65, and 67 (note there is no 65A) which had therefore been recently built by him. He made provision for a ground rent payable for 999 years, this would not have been possible had Robert's property existed already on the site, because Robert had paid a ground rent of £7 13s. from 3rd. November 1789, term 999 years.

On 19th February 1810 William leased the two properties 63 and 65 Roe Street to Nathaniel Pearson, and this is where the possible Wesleyan connection has arisen, because in earlier years the Pearson family were instrumental in promoting Methodism and very

Roe Street Nos. 63-67 but notice the doorway for 65A spoiling the symmetry of the original house at no. 67 on the right.

much involved with John Wesley's visits to the town. However, John Wesley had died in 1791 having last visited Macclesfield in April 1790, so it is not possible for him to have stayed on Roe St.

At the same time as the Pearson lease began No. 67 was let to Samuel Stone, a surgeon, who became involved with the sale of the Macclesfield brass works in 1813, of which William Roe still held a considerable interest. The decision to sell the works, built in 1774 adjacent to what is now the lower south side of Windmill Street, had been taken in 1801, after production had ceased.

This was the time of the Napoleonic Wars when economic stagnation was becoming widespread, so the sale of the premises and site took several years to complete. Nothing was ever wasted and I suspect that William Roe used fittings from the office of the brass works to furnish No. 67 Roe Street e.g. copper fireplaces which would have acted as a great advertisement for anyone visiting the works on the Common.

Official records at this period were badly kept, as evidenced by the haphazard way in which the Macclesfield Land Tax Returns were completed, tonnage in the River Weaver books recorded, and even the collation of information for the first census of 1801. The latter was disputed by contemporaries who judged the population to be far greater than that recorded – all the result of conscientious well-educated clerks going to war and being replaced in a hurry!

By 1820, with the war over, the desire for meticulous records had returned and suddenly many more street names are listed for Macclesfield, including Roe Street. William Roe was still in possession of the Roe Street property, but with an interesting addition. Samuel Stone still tenanted No. 67, the tax payable 3s. 9d. Next was a small property for William Roe's own use, tax payable of 4d. only and must relate to the unit created out of 67 i.e. 65A, but probably only the ground floor at that time. The other two properties, now 63 and 65, are shown as a multiple letting to Thomas Stubbs, John Barker & others, total tax 2s. There is no connection between Robert Roe and this group of properties.

The second item relates to the 'Historical Background' of John de Macclesfield Snr. as presented in a recently published booklet *Macclesfield's Great Place*, part of which seems an incredible conjecture, that he was a priest and son of John Alcock Snr.

According to Bruell's thorough research, John de M. refused to take Holy Orders in 1391 which led to differences with Pope Boniface IX. The John de M. ordained in 1378 appears to have become chaplain of Denham in Bucks, on 12th August 1387 and acted in a legal capacity for John Snr. on several occasions; they were obviously closely related.

Bruell also questions the assumption that he was the son of Alcock Snr. and I agree. There were two brothers Adam and William de Macclesfield at the time of Edward I and Queen Eleanor, and Eleanor's bailiff Thomas de M. had at least two brothers, Richard and John, the latter a magistrate of Chester. Although Thomas's heirs died out I suspect, like the historian Ormerod, that John Snr. was descended from the Chester branch; his grandfather was a William.

Bruell points out that there appears to be an error on the latin deed relating to a Macclesfield property.

The Wallgate property was conveyed by Roger Ballesone to John Alcock & heir (i.e. John Jnr,) in 1363. After the father's death the son borrowed money in 1373 from John de Cliff and presumably could not repay, for in 1385 Cliff tried to claim the land. John Alcock Jnr. managed to hold on to the property, confirmed by deed of 24th June 1385 but in doing so had evidently borrowed more money from the Dounes family to pay off the debt, using several properties as collateral.

In 1391, 'the great money lender' and important civil servant John de M. Snr. stepped in and acquired the properties, the deed qualifying them as previously belonging to John Alcock Snr., – his father, hence the confusion. But an earlier deed of 1385 translates as John Alcock Snr., – the father, to distinguish him from his son who had by then inherited.

Also in 1435 John de M. Snr's nearest legitimate heir was recorded as his kinsman Roger Legh – one of William de M.'s female descendants had married into the Legh family. John Alcock Jnr. left an heiress, so where does this place John de M. Snr?

The Tudor fireplace at Little Moreton Hall with the coat of arms commemorating the marriage of John de Morton to Margaret de Macclesfield in 1329. Courtesy of The National Trust.

Christmas – Egypt and Marianne Brocklehurst

Amongst the books published in time for Christmas 1891 was one entitled *Pharaohs, Fellahs and Explorers* by Amelia B. Edwards (pub. Osgood McIlvaine & Co.) 'the indefatigable honorary secretary' of the Egypt Exploration Fund. But why should this particular person be of interest, or indeed have any connection with Macclesfield?

The first clue lies in the fact that the merest mention of Egyptology should bring out a sense of pride in all Maxonians, for in our midst at the West Park (formerly Brocklehurst) Museum is housed one of the finest Egyptian collections in Europe, and that according to a German professor from Munich University who visited some years ago when I was on duty.

The West Park Museum adjacent to Prestbury Road, formerly known as the Brocklehurst Museum. It was built and endowed by Miss Marianne Brocklehurst with the help of her brother, Peter Pownall Brocklehurst, both members of the famous silk family which rose to prominence during the 19th century. The museum was opened in October 1898 and celebrated its centenary in 1998. It is open daily from 1.30 p.m. to 4.00 p.m.

Despite having only one comparatively small mummy in the collection, its pristine condition singles it out as a remarkable asset when compared with the condition of those in other museums.

Many readers will be familiar with the story of how Marianne Brocklehurst (daughter of John Brocklehurst of Hurdsfield House) travelled to Egypt in 1873 and during her expedition acquired several of the items now on display. What might not be so well-known is the fact that during her 'grand tour' she met Miss Amelia Edwards on board the ship sailing for Alexandria.

The Edwards and Brocklehurst parties were to meet on several occasions during their respective arab boat journeys along the Nile, in fact Marianne and her friend were invited on board Amelia's boat for 'a state dinner' on Christmas Day. These boats although comparatively small (having sleeping accommodation for about seven passengers) were nevertheless, adequately equipped. The festivities were evidently a jolly affair with champagne and a 'large blazing plum pudding' for dessert, whilst the crew presented lively entertainment with one of their number proving to be a gifted comedian.

Miss Edwards, an excellent artist and draughtswoman, was also a writer and author of several books, one of which gives an account of the 1873 expedition and where appropriate, mentions Marianne's involvement. Originally published in 1877, *One Thousand Miles up the Nile* warranted a Second Edition in 1889.

Marianne undertook two further visits to Egygt during the winter seasons of 1882-83 and 1890-91 and continued her assiduous purchases of antiquities from market stalls, bazaars etc. which must have given her the idea and desire to put on display these fascinating objects so that the general public, and in particular the residents of Macclesfield, could enjoy at first hand her unusual collection.

Her eventual idea was to build a museum for the town with the dual purpose of fostering education and interest; and where better to build than in one of the earliest municipal parks in the country, where bowling and tearooms were already attracting a large part of the community. With help from her brother, Peter Pownall Brocklehurst, she completed the task in 1898, but only lived for a few weeks after the opening ceremony in October of that year.

Fortunately Marianne had earlier informed Amelia Edwards of her ambitious intentions, with the result that other items were generously donated by the Egypt Exploration Fund to supplement Marianne's collection. Again these are part of the display e.g. a pair of leather boots with pointed toes and leather soles, with the uppers punched for stitching and dating from the late Ptolemaic Period. (The last Ptolemy was the son of Julius Caesar and Cleopatra who ruled with his mother from 45 B.C. to 30 B.C.).

Concern for her own personal collection is reflected in Marianne's

Miss Amelia Edwards 'the indefatigable honorary secretary' of the Egypt Exploration Fund who, through her friendship with Marianne Brocklehurst, was instrumental in providing many of the antiquities on display at the West Park Museum.

Will, for she bequeathed it to her great-niece, the Duchess of Yarborough, who in turn donated it to the museum.

Whilst Marianne was preparing for her third and final trip to Egypt in 1890, Amelia Edwards was busy touring America and subsequently produced her lectures as a series of essays in her new book for Christmas 1891.

The newspaper review records that ' The 'explorers' direct the excavations, the 'fellahs' are the labourers, and together they discover the 'Pharaohs, their palaces, their cities, and even the homely details of their kitchens and sculleries'.

One chapter which was singled out as 're-markable' concerned portrait-painting in ancient Egypt and showed the influence it had on early Greek artists. The sixth chapter related to Egyptian literature, whilst the seventh explained 'the hieroglyphic writing and language in perhaps the most lucid manner possible for such a difficult subject'.

Whilst Amelia's strong character and dogged persistence for conservation and seeking the truth sometimes brought her into direct conflict with one or two of her male contemporaries (some things never change!), yet the Illustrated London News was more than happy to promote her cause, declaring:

'Indeed, we know of no account so attractive and useful for those who are anxious to get clear ideas as to the origin and history of picture writing'. And in conclusion:

'The book is furnished with an excellent index, and forms a most attractive addition to popular works on Egyptology.'

This was marketing done with great decorum and although the reviewer stopped short of writing it, one can almost hear him saying, 'and a jolly good Christmas stocking filler too!'

The Name 'Macclesfield'

It is almost a millennium ago since the name of Macclesfield significantly entered the records, with the inference of an earlier establishment. The name appears in the Domesday Survey as 'Maclesfeld' but in many early records has various spellings, a popular one being 'Maklesfeld'.

A hunting party similar to those frequenting Macclesfield Forest in the Early Renaissance Period.

In considering the name there are two choices; a) that someone with a surname of Macclesfield settled here and the place adopted the name, as in the case of Sutton or Langley; b) the locality was already known as Maclesfeld and someone then chose the name as his surname in preference to his trade or profession. As Macclesfield is a unique (early) name then choice b) must be preferred.

In Old English (Anglo-Saxon) feld or felde is field so we could expect the Macles part also to be Anglo-Saxon. Previously it has been deduced that as Macca was a Saxon personal surname, this was probably its origin.

There is another strong possibility, suggested to me when I was searching for a similar name in Germany, the old meaning of the German (Saxon) word 'Makler' is trader, (today it relates to a broker i.e. middle man, sometimes it can be translated as estate agent or even stock-broker) and this seems a feasible alternative.

The survey, undertaken for a Norman/French king is written in Latin but the letter 'k' is a rarity in both French and Latin so a clerk writing down the details would be more inclined to use a c than a k.

Cheshire had two important commodities, cheese and salt. The former was said to have been introduced by the Romans and the latter produced by them. There is a record of the saltworks in Cheshire at the time of Edward the Confessor (1042-1066), and so important had they become (apart from a temporary decline, presumably due to the ravages of war) that Domesday details every aspect of production.

Macclesfield was at the heart of the salt routes eastwards from the Wiches; one led through Whaley Bridge via Saltgate Lane to Sheffield. Two alternative routes via Buxton passed Salter's Flatt, Saltersford (no. 2) and Tideswell from where again options were open to travel either to Chesterfield (via Saltergate) or Sheffield (via Salter's Ford, Salter Sitch and Psalter Lane).

There was an important northern route from Northwich to Stockport and then into what had earlier been the wealthy and cultured county of Yorkshire, that is until the Viking invasion of 866 when, on 1st November York was overrun and the society in the vast surrounding area was totally annihilated.

A salt route to the south of Macclesfield ran from the Wiches, converged on Congleton and continued to Chesterfield or Nottingham.

The routes through Macclesfield must have been by far the most difficult, even for pack-horses, and yet they would have been more secure in times of trouble e.g. when marauding Norsemen made periodic incursions into the Mersey Estuary, burning and pillaging the shoreline settlements.

Salt was, of course, almost as precious as gold and also heavy to transport. Sometimes it was carried by oxcart in addition to packhorses and Macclesfield would have been an ideal site for merchants to meet, where loads could be split up and sold, then distributed over a significant area; likewise the cheeses. It is an interesting thought, therefore, that the name of Macclesfield could have signified the field of the trader.

This also fits more comfortably with the name Hyrdesfeld (Hurdsfield) for hierde in West Saxon means a shepherd, guardian or keeper and it is known that Thomas of Macclesfield (the late 13th century bailiff of Queen Eleanor) had an enclosure for animals in that area; a tradition probably carried on from earlier times.

The next intruiging question is why Macclesfield appears as a manor in the Hameston Hundred if they were the same place, (the deduction held to date is that Macclesfield had changed its name from Hamestan).

The Normans reorganised the county into 12 hundreds; by 1360 it was reduced to 7. Before Domesday?; pure speculation – but 5 have been contrived. The hundreds appear in the reign of Edgar, the first Anglo-Saxon King of England (959-975) but no one really knows what a hundred represents. The Norman's 12 covered 1,200 hides (a measure of land) and hints at 100 hides per hundred.

One idea for the pre-Conquest division is an ecclesiastical basis, whilst another is based on an old German tradition of dividing land into areas, each capable of providing 100 men for military service. Hamestan, although the largest in area, was next to last in size of population, and there is no indication that it had ever been anything but an insignificant barren marshy area.

The Danes had predominantly occupied areas with access to the sea e.g. Chester, the Wirral and along the Mersey Estuary – they were farmers and fishermen.

However, the Normans were the great forest administrators, hence the concentration of power in Macclesfield and the subsequent intensive development of the area. This implies that Hamestan was a different place in a much larger hundred from which the Macclesfield Hundred was formed.

Doneham (Dunham Massey) has proved to be a very important site, confirmed by recent archaeologi-cal digs. It was just far enough from the Mersey not to suffer the periodic rapid raids of pirates; but with the great Viking invasion of the 9th century was probably laid waste. Yet by 1087 it had recovered sufficiently to have a house in the 'city', (? Chester), which certainly indicates an important link with county administration; it was also on the important salt route into Yorkshire, so, could this have been the site of Hamestan? William I created a barony there, which suggests compensation for some reason to Hamon de Mascy; perhaps he was expecting a more lucrative role in the hundred administration but found part of his territory taken away.

This was, of course, before the creation of the borough of Macclesfield, so the land claimed would have been manor and forest, which needed special attention.

This leads to yet another mystery. The borough was created (by tradition in 1220) in Macclesfield, not Prestbury where the church stood. Guilds always adopted a saint and regularly attended church. The Prestbury church and land had been granted to St. Werburgh's abbey at Chester by the Earl of Chester, so in aptly choosing the nearest piece of defensible land least suited to agriculture, a nearby soil eroded windswept hilltop was chosen and the Borough of Macclesfield was born.

The entrance to Dunham Massey – could this have been the former Hamestan?

161

Plague

In this country today can anyone really imagine the horror and fear of a plague? Our nearest taste of the reality is recent 'flu' epidemics when everyone, even if they did not succumb to it themselves, knew someone who had. The fear amongst the elderly must have been the most pronounced; but the plagues of the past knew no bounds of age or status when instilling fear (although the more affluent had the means to take themselves away from the rest of society for a period and had a greater resistance due to a more substantial diet).

The death head (symbolic of the plague) in the stonework of the gateway of St. James the Great, Gawsworth.

What could be worse than an almost guaranteed miserable and horrible way to die? So therefore imagine if all those people who have recently suffered influenza, instead had been plague victims and not survived; how would it have affected your lives and mine? Out of my immediate family members of nine, four would have perished, and based on available (but scanty) information this just – over 50% survival rate is what has been judged to relate to England during the years of 'Pestilence' i.e. 1348-49, 1360 and 1379.

The previous century (13th) had witnessed remarkable advances in art, culture, knowledge and religion. Many religious houses and hospitals had been established and endowments made to cathedrals, churches and the university colleges of Oxford and Cambridge.

Suddenly disaster struck and those living in close communities, especially the religious monasteries and priories, where the brethren were administering to the sick and dying, were the most affected. Where records have survived, as on the Continent, the effect was quite startling. One Dominican priory in the German town of Osnabrueck, which had been the keystone for the administration of education, nursing the sick and so forth, lost ninety of its members.

And whereas these religious establishments had been able to operate in a self-sufficient manner using the talents of their members, now this was no longer possible. Many of the secular duties of the priests were taken over by lay people; this was a unique period. The greatest responsibility would have been to keep the accounts and collect revenues and one can well imagine that only those with a good education, knowledgeable in law and known to be honest men, would have qualified for such positions.

After the decimation of the ecclesiastical society in the mid-14th century it would take at least two generations to recover, and it is interesting to note that the parliament of 1371 compelled Edward III to dismiss all his clerical ministers etc. and replace them with laymen. Now the secular world would encroach, and feelings of resentment were bound to be fuelled by a realisation of the 'hidden' wealth of the Church.

* * *

In the aftermath of the first great 'Visitation' of the plague John of Macclesfield was born. On 31st October 1417 he wrote a letter stating he was 'sixty-six years and more, broken by age and infirmity', suggesting a date of birth about 1350/51 and a very hard life! At his death his grandfather's name was recorded as William, but unfortunately the document is damaged where his father's name should appear.

Firstly I want to consider the long held view that John of Macclesfield must have been a priest 'and was unable to marry Katherine Kingsley for that reason'.

In his forties John was employed as a civil servant of Richard II in the Privy Seal and Signet offices in London and would be described as 'clerici senioris' – a senior clerk. Whilst clerk in the usual sense meant a cleric, this really denoted a person of learning i.e. a scholar, and since it was almost always the clergy who were educated and did most of the reading and writing, the words were virtually synonymous, but not quite.

John was therefore not described as 'presbyter qui ecclesiae servit' (an elder of the Christian Church), a 'sacerdos' (priest) nor 'clericus ecclesiae' (a clerk of the church) but a senior clerk – as indeed he was, in royal service, and there were not too many of those around. He was a very learned man, for when he died his will contained the details of a small but important library. He was part of a group of extremely 'able men' e.g. Edmund Stafford, Keeper of the Privy Seal from 1389 to 1396 (at which date he became Chancellor), was a man well trained in Roman Law and John also must have had a good understanding of it.

The study of law was a tradition in the Macclesfield family. From the days of Thomas of Macclesfield, Queen Eleanor's forest bailiff, the family members had proved themselves competent in holding such positions. Thomas's son, Jordan, continued his studies at Oxford for a further three years to become expert in canon and civil law, and Jordan's son was Justice of the Forest of Wirral and a magistrate (presumably in Chester). Even Thomas's brother John was a magistrate and again this appears to have been in Chester.

At one stage in his career John of Macclesfield was Rector of Barrow, but this too can be regarded in a lay sense as he was probably collecting tythes in the aftermath of the plague. Even his lucrative sinecure as provost of Wells Cathedral from 7th December 1389 does not require him to have taken Holy Orders at that time. This would have been a reward for services rendered.

* * *

When the Black Prince, father of Richard II, involved himself with the Cheshire administration after years of its semi-independence, he made sure that a committee based in London oversaw his territory whilst he was away campaigning in France. He desperately needed money to fund his overseas ventures and could no longer present his favourites with manors and lands, so alternatives were sought, such as life annuities etc. a situation which continued for some time.

The Black Prince died the year before his father, so Richard II was a young boy of only ten years when he succeeded to the throne in 1377 and had to rely on his magnates, ministers and secretaries to remain loyal and carry out their duties honourably. He married Anne of Luxembourg on 14th January 1382, which was a good marriage, as Anne was the daughter of the Holy Roman Emperor, Charles IV, King of Bohemia.

Many intrigues were afoot and on 1st October 1386 the Chancellor, William de la Pole was impeached and imprisoned. On 8th September 1387 one of Richard's two dearest friends, Robert de Vere, was appointed Justiciar of Cheshire and this could be significant in the John of Macclesfield story. It is important to note that Richard seized personal power in a coup on 3rd May 1389, and as John was appointed Provost of Wells Cathedral in December of that year, it surely must have been a reward for loyalty and good service.

Detail from the Wilton Diptych of Richard II (National Gallery London). Each figure is wearing the badge of the white hart, widely distributed by Richard as his emblem, and part of an elaborate court dress which John of Macclesfield would have worn as a civil servant.

John de Macclesfield Part I

The Early Years

John of Macclesfield has always remained something of an intriguing and elusive character, almost a man of myths and legends, inspiring me to continue exploring further the circumstantial evidence relating to his early years, in the hope of learning more about him.

A person very rarely stands alone, so it is important to look at associates, family and friends in finding clues to their identity, and the indications are that John was born and brought up in Chester.

At the time of his birth (1350/51), Edward, Prince of Wales (the Black Prince) apart from his Duchy lands etc. held Chester as Earl together with the Manor and Forest of Macclesfield, and had two salaried officials only in Cheshire: the chamberlain and the escheator.

From 1352 the escheator acted as steward of the desmesne manors and towns of the earldom, and by 1354 all the chief county officials received salaries and held their offices 'at the prince's pleasure', but the administration was overseen from London. This meant that auditors were periodically sent to inspect the accounts; the Black Prince, however, was a fair and generous man and those who served him well were rewarded accordingly.

Peter Lacy, receiver-general of Cheshire from 1346 to 1371 was also keeper of the King's Privy Seal (Edward III) during the last four years of his receivership.

Sir Hugh Segrave, who in 1372 was acting as steward in Cheshire, became steward of Richard II's household during his minority (1378/81) and treasurer of England (1381/86) and was one of the Keepers of the Great Seal in 1382.

Therefore if you served well as a senior civil servant in Cheshire, promotion was possible in London.

Another way in which the Black Prince granted favours was by giving valuable oak trees as gifts from his forests. Usually it was two, but sometimes four, mostly from the forest of Lyme in Macclesfield Hundred. In November 1354 four oaks were sent to the Archdeacon of Richmond in Yorkshire. In May 1357 and in May 1358 on each occasion two oaks were sent to individuals for repairs to their houses, again as gifts from the prince for services rendered.

But one gift is interesting: on 13th September 1358 a writ was made out 'to deliver to Adam de

An English oak. Many 'fit for timber' were taken from Lyme forest on the orders of the Black Prince and given as gifts to various individuals, usually for good service.

Kyngeslegh two oaks fit for timber in the wood of Lyme'. No qualification is given, as in every other instance i.e. that they were for building or repairing purposes. Also, as some of the other trees were sent great distances, the whereabouts of Kyngeslegh cannot be confirmed; he could have been living in the Macclesfield area but not necessarily. (His son and heir, John, later held property in Nantwich).

This is the man whose daughter would eventually provide John of Macclesfield with six illegitimate children, but at this early date John was only 8 years old.

Meanwhile on 4th December 1361 the prince approved Kyngeslegh's appointment as escheator of Cheshire and steward of foreign courts, which suggests that at that time he was living in Chester.

* * *

Kyngeslegh was proving to be an excellent civil servant for on 21st November 1365 the prince's lieutenant and auditors were ordered to inspect the rolls of sessions of the three 'justices of labourers' in the hundred of Macclesfield i.e. Robert de Legh, John Davenport and Adam de

Kyngeslegh, and give them rewards for the profits they had made for the prince.

At present the earliest recorded deed for Kyngeslegh acquiring property in Macclesfield in that dated 18th November 1376 in Wallgate, which does suggest that it was an investment. The opportunity had probably arisen for the acquisition because of his connections in the area.

Where did Kyngeslegh come from? And how did he manage to secure his appointment in the prince's employ in Chester?

One important fact to remember is that Cheshire was part of the (Coventry and) Lichfield Diocese, together with Staffordshire, Derbyshire, south Lancashire, north Shropshire, north and west Warwickshire, a few parishes in Flintshire and one in Denbighshire – a considerable ecclesiastical area. There was a great cohesion in the diocese not only amongst the religious community but also within the guilds and therefore trades etc. and the hierarchy controlling the different strands of society often 'overlapped'.

The Holy Trinity

Coventry was an extremely important city, famous for its woollen trade, and at that period one of its greatest patrons was the Black Prince. In the early 1340s, three guilds had been founded which amalgamated with a fourth, the Holy Trinity (of 1364) to receive Letters Patent from Richard II in 1392. The name Holy Trinity is an obvious indicator of the Black Prince's involvement, and the guilds produced a flourishing trade in woollen cloth, caps and bonnets by the turn of the century.

Although chronological, unfortunately the records of guild members are without dates; Kyngeslegh with wife Ellen appear very early (page 4); John of Macclesfield is listed on page 45.

In September 1402 there is a deed for a plot of land near the Macclesfield market place in which Kyngeslegh had earlier held an interest. It passed to a group of individuals including John Whitchirche of Coventry, merchant, then came into the possession of John of Macclesfield (who tranferred it to

his namesake the parson of Denham as trustee). The connection has to be the woollen trade.

Also at this period there was an acre of land in Hurdsfield called le 'Trinite'. In 1893 when Fence House was being demolished to make way for Fence Ave., the ruins of a mediaeval building were discovered, and on a broken piece of plasterwork was the emblem of the Trinity. John de Macclesfield gave Kyngeslegh land in Hurdsfield which seems to indicate a source of income for the Coventry guild, possibly where the sheep were kept for shearing. Today the church of Holy Trinity, Hurdsfield is a reminder of the mediaeval guild of merchants who cared for their sick and bereaved members and supported each other financially and with prayers.

Holy Trinity church, Hurdsfield together with its graveyard are more than likely on the site of the 14th century 'land of the Holy Trinity' relating to a very important guild in Coventry to which many important people belonged.

The Macclesfield Family

In the mid-14th century, when John of Macclesfield was born, there was still a member of the Macclesfield family owning property in Macclesfield. He was yet another John, and grandson of Thomas, Queen Eleanor's forest bailiff, but he died in 1369 leaving no heir, so his lands etc. passed to his nephew, Richard de Moreton (son of his sister Margaret).

This John had held the position of justice in the forest of Wirral, and as the family had a residence in Flintshire, he would have used this as his base. In fact his father, Jordan, when studying at Oxford University in February 1308 is described as of Worthenbury, Flintshire, not Macclesfield.

Yet John, the Wirral justice, did not forsake his ties with the township of Macclesfield for he was mayor in 1358/59, although the population was very much depleted because of the plague some eight or nine years earlier. In fact the Black Prince, whilst visiting the manor on 21st November 1359, 'made out a letter in favour of John de Maclesfeld' evidently in answer to a petition received from John on the previous 3rd June when mayor. Unfortunately the subject of this correspondence is not known.

Christian names were extremely important in family relationships until quite recently; apart from the name, John, another significant Christian name in the Macclesfield family was William, and very much connected with Chester.

One is mentioned doing war service in Wales for Edward I and would have been contemporary with Thomas, the Macclesfield forest bailiff (late 13th century). A little earlier this William held the bedelry of the Hundred of

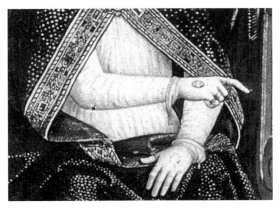

Detail from a mid-15th century fresco depicting Pope Pius II wearing a pair of white gloves, part of his accoutrements of high office.

Macclesfield i.e. he held the office of justice for the whole hundred and would be responsible for implementing new laws and carrying out instructions from the Chester administration.

Yet another (possibly the son of the aforementioned William) was a Dominican friar described as 'probably Chester Convent'; he died in 1303; in 1345 there is a mention of a William of Macclesfield, citizen of Chester; finally our subject John of Macclesfield (of 'Castle' fame) named his first son and heir, John, after himself but his second son, William, which by Christian tradition would normally be after his father or his wife's father. The mother of these sons was Katherine de Kyngeslegh whose father was named Adam, so one would expect William to have been named after his paternal grandfather.

It can be seen, therefore, that the Macclesfield family connections with the county town of Chester were significant, and this would have been absolutely essential in order to develop strong ties with royal officials enabling family members to hold on to their prestigious positions and in the hope of gaining higher office.

* * *

It is not unreasonable to suggest that our subject John of Macclesfield as a young man was trained in the escheator's office in Chester, where he met and was aided by Adam de Kyngeslegh. Kyngeslegh was, of course, in Chester by 1361 when he was appointed by the prince as escheator, a position which he would hold on other occasions during a further 40 years service; he was also sheriff of Flint in 1383. There seems little doubt that Kyngeslegh had gained his post because of his membership of the Coventry Guild and in the not too distant future John of Macclesfield would himself become a member.

Kyngeslegh would have known the previous John of Macclesfield (Mayor in 1358) and it is this John who for the three years 1366-68 charged a Henry Dyot with an unusual quit rent on part of his Macclesfield property i.e. a pair of white gloves for each year. It is an interesting thought that the idea might have been aided by Kyngeslegh, for where occupations are shown for Holy Trinity Guild members in Coventry, glovers are included.

Variations in the spelling of names often complicates research and this is probably why Kyngeslegh has been difficult to trace. However, in the guild records his name appears as

Kyndesly which suggests that he was a member of the Kinardsly family of Hereford, entitled to bear a Coat of Arms which was adapted by the minor branches as they spread across the Midlands into Staffordshire and Derbyshire.

By 1300 one branch was established at Loxley near Uttoxeter, but from which branch Adam came is at present not known. One undisputed point is that Hereford was famous for glove making, a tradition which would last for centuries despite various unsuccessful attempts to introduce a woollen industry.

* * *

Medieval gloves were 'a symbol of authority as well as of feudal investiture'. The giving of a glove emphasised trust, and conversely if a glove was thrown or used to strike someone, it was indicative of mistrust from which a duel usually ensued.

Gloves made in the 13th century were either of iron for soldiers, or leather, many of the latter being reinforced for falconry. Wealthy women soon acquired them made from silk, hemp, fur and, of course, leather.

There were strict rules governing the wearing of gloves, particularly for lesser mortals. They could not be worn in church or when saluting, dancing or paying homage, or at any time in the presence of a feudal lord.

Today a pair of white gloves would be significant as part of a uniform, so from that point of view the tradition has remained. They were obviously significant to John of Macclesfield and would have been an expensive item, and were possibly connected with his position as a forest justice.

When this John died, Edward III was still reigning and the Black Prince was keeping tight control over his revenues from his possessions in Cornwall, Cheshire and Wales through the employ of his professional administrators. His various household departments were therefore conversant with matters in all these areas and there would have been much coming and going amongst the Prince's personnel. It is not surprising to find links between men from Macclesfield and the other areas, links which again have occurred from time to time over the centuries because of the royal possessions.

Quite suddenly an important change took place with the unexpected death of the Black Prince and on 13th October 1376 the chamberlain of Chester was ordered to give his widow, Princess Joan lands in Cheshire as a portion of her dower.

Detail from an Italian fresco circa 1400 showing the typical female costume of the period also popular in England. Note the gloves.

Promotion

At the time of the Black Prince's death in 1376 John of Macclesfield was a young man of about 26 years of age and had not yet emerged from the shadows.

The Prince's widow, Joan, was reputed to be one of the most beautiful women in England, and also quite wealthy, being countess of Kent in her own right. Nevertheless she was granted a dower totalling £2,500 which included the Prince's Cheshire lands, in addition to which she had her own lands in Kent. One year later, on the death of Edward III, she was to acquire considerable influence as the mother of the nine-year-old king, Richard II.

Sadly her premature death in 1385 only added to a worsening situation, as 'the powers that be' conspired against each other for control during the young king's minority. Already unrest had spread to the lower classes, as bands of rebels from Kent and Essex marched on London during the Peasants Revolt of 1381.

On 20th February 1386 the executors of Joan's Will granted Macclesfield manor, lordship and hundred (including custody of the forest) to Dame Joan de Mohun, and the leasing of the park demesne to John of Macclesfield. King Richard confirmed the grant of the manor to Dame Joan on 5th June 1386, but in November 1389 she allowed Richard's wife, Anne, to become Lady of the Manor together with all its perquisites, in exchange for a payment of £100 per annum.

About the time of the Peasants Revolt John of Macclesfield, by then over 30 years of age, enters the records as rector of Talkarn (Tolcarn), Cornwall (some time between1381-85), and as it is not recorded in the bishop's register it does suggest a lay position.

As the Black Prince's administration was responsible for all the revenues of Cheshire and Cornwall etc. it is not surprising that a clerk from the Cheshire administration would be able to take up just such a vacant rectory; the Prince, of course, was also Duke of Cornwall and Prince of Wales in addition to Earl of Chester.

It is interesting to note that the Mohun family had a close association with Cornwall and Lady Mohun, a kinswoman of Richard II, had quite an influence at Court. Had John of Macclesfield become known to her because of the Cornish connection and as a consequence put her in a position to be able to acquire the Macclesfield grant? (Perhaps with prompting from Kyngeslegh who knew how lucrative the Macclesfield holding could be). Was his permitted leasing of the park demesne a reward for such a service? We may never know, but the circumstantial evidence is strong, and it is the interweaving of personalities such as these which makes history so fascinating.

There are also other indicators to suggest that the wool trade was a common interest. Mohun, as the variant Mouen, is the name of a family near Ghent in Flanders in the early 15th century and not too far from Brabant. The area had a considerable trade with England and was famous for dyeing wool (the uncle of Anne, Richard's wife, was Duke of Brabant and on her way to marry Richard she had visited him); and John of Macclefield, in leasing the park, had gained the facility of 'the Lord's fold' which seems to indicate the breeding of sheep.

With his feet now firmly on the ladder, John of Macclesfield began his rapid ascent, acquiring firstly the rectories of Denham in Buckinghamshire and Mackworth in Derbyshire. He would acquire others during his career, but all only for short periods, as though in a caretaker capacity of tidying-up the books, collecting arrears and placing accounts on a firm basis to enable a chaplain to take over. England was still recovering from the ravages of the plague.

The rectory of Denham might sound somewhat obscure and remote, but it belonged to the Benedictine monastery of St. Peter's, Westminster, better known to us today as Westminster Abbey; and although John held the rectory for only a short period to 12th August 1387, when his namesake and presumably close relative became parson, it was another extremely important link in the chain.

* * *

Henry III (1216-1272) had spent considerable sums on the Benedictine monastery at Westminster and established the Law Courts there, encouraging early Parliaments in the Chapter House and cloisters, so it took on a political as well as religious significance. By the 14th century the monks had a superb library with bookcases lining the walls of the North Cloister, and John would certainly have made good use of his connections there.

His relationship with the Benedictines seems to have been fairly strong, suggesting an early involvement with St. Werburgh's abbey in Chester, now Chester Cathedral. This abbey was extremely wealthy, and amongst its possessions was the valuable church of Prestbury, granted to the abbey by Hugh II, Earl of Chester, between June 1181 and October 1182. It is possibly, because of this grant, that the borough was established in Macclesfield, not Prestbury, allowing the Earl the revenue and not the abbot.

A young monk called Ranulf Higden entered St. Werburgh's in 1299 and died there in 1363, when John was about 13 years of age. This

An unusual view of Westminster Abbey taken in the 1930s. This was originally a great Benedictine abbey, a seat of learning and the place where politics first established itself alongside religion.

Norman doorway with tympanum, Prestbury. A church once granted to the wealthy Benedictine abbey of St. Werbugh, Chester.

monk became famous for his great work, a history of the world from its creation to 1327, which he eventually completed to 1352. The book was entitled *Polychronicon* and was copied and purchased mostly by monsteries, churches and wealthy individuals, for it was extremely expensive. It was later added to by others and was amongst the early books to be printed by Caxton.

In between the shorter version and the extended ones, Higden enlarged his own copy to 1352, but it was not popular because everyone had already bought the earlier version; so apart from Higden's copy, only two other copies of this version are known, one belonged to Christ Church, Canterbury and the other to John of Macclesfield.

Surprisingly John lent his copy to the abbot of Chester on 5th August 1416; one has to wonder why. What had happened to St. Werburgh's (i.e. Higden's) own copy – which has been judged to have remained there until the Dissolution? Certainly he must have known the abbot, Thomas Erdeley, very well indeed.

From the first glimpse of John of Macclesfield he begins to appear as a charmer amongst the

ladies, and confident enough to take his place amongst those who were part of the cultural court of Richard II, who himself adored books. John began his own collection, an expensive hobby. But how he acquired the Polychronicon is intriguing; it could have been in lieu of payment for services rendered on behalf of St. Werburgh's and maybe in connection with St. Peter's, Prestbury.

The Parkland

Before continuing with John of Macclesfield's incredible career during a very turbulent period of English history, it is appropriate to consider the role of the Alcock family in relation to Macclesfield.

In the year 1355 the parkland of Macclesfield was supporting a large herd of cattle, which would reach over 700 head by 1363, and all belonging to Edward of Woodstock, nicknamed 'The Black Prince' by the Victorians. His continental campaigns required considerable financing and equipment, so he needed administrators who were trustworthy, reliable and loyal to manage his large estates during his absences.

In January 1355 Edward had made an interesting request to have 'more cow-houses' in Macclesfield forest and to increase his stock there. At this time he was involved in building works at his manor of 'Kenyngton' (today site of the Surrey cricket ground, Kennington Oval, and still owned by the Prince of Wales). The funding for this project was to be collected from the Cheshire revenue, and he therefore ordered his auditors to 'look round for some other foreign parcel of money' and then inform him of the amount; he would then give the order to increase the stock. The money was found and the plan went ahead.

Surrey Cricket Ground, The Oval, (early 1990s) with its famous gasometer. This was originally the site of Kennington Palace built by Edward, Prince of Wales (the Black Prince) with the aid of Cheshire revenue in the mid-14th century. Today the land is still owned by the Prince of Wales.

At this time Alexander Crosse of Prestwich, who had only been the Prince's stock-keeper in Cheshire for one year, petitioned the prince for an increase in wages because of the extra work involved, not only for himself but also his groom. This was a time of unrest in many areas and Alexander, for some unknown reason, was 'greatly afraid of the peril of fire in his absence', which seems to indicate that he was afraid of his household in Lancashire being attacked whilst he was on duty in Cheshire. In the circumstances it was agreed that if he chose not to live in Macclesfield manor he could have a small house, built for himself somewhere in the region, at the Prince's expense.

By May the Prince was preparing for war in France and, although his mind was on other matters, he sent strict instructions to Robert de Legh (deputy steward of Macclesfield forest) that he had to safeguard the Prince's interests during his absence overseas. The stock farm in Macclesfield suddenly found itself in the hands of a John Alcock who, according to instructions, began to build up the herd.

Where did this Alcock appear from? Certainly not from Lancashire, as his predecessor, but the indications are that he came from the Midlands like Adam de Kyngeslegh

The Alcock Family

In the early 1500s the Alcocks can be traced in Northants, and there was also a branch at Hanbury in Staffs. Even earlier, circa 1400 and contemporary with John of Macclesfield, one called William was a burgess of Kingston-upon-Hull. This neatly fits the pattern of many mercantile families in the Midlands who traded with the Continent via the port of Hull, and used the River Trent for transporting their goods. Hull had important links, not only with London, but with ports such as Hamburg, and a merchant would send a close relative, usually a son or nephew, to Hull in order to oversee business matters there.

William Alcock had a son born 1430 named John who rose to fame; not only did he become Bishop of Rochester, followed by Worcester then Ely, but was a brilliant architect, becoming comptroller of the royal works and buildings for Henry VII. He was also tutor to young Edward V for a period.

The Alcocks, therefore, were not an insignificant family and, like the Kyngesleghs, were entitled to a Coat of Arms. The John Alcock who arrived in Macclesfield must have been recommended for the post and must have had considerable experience in cattle breeding. The Ferrers family held lands in Staffordshire, despite one of their ancestors forfeiting the Earl of Derby title, together with vast estates and Tutbury Castle. Some pride had been regained when Sir Thomas, justiciar of Chester, had also held the additional post of steward and bailiff of Macclesfield manor in 1348 before the arrival of the plague; he died in 1353. Perhaps the Staffordshire connection and the presence of the Prince's personnel at Channock Chase, one of his favourite hunting grounds, could provide the answer.

Unfortunately for John Alcock, the triumph of Poitiers spelt misfortune for him because the Black Prince appointed William Chorley in his stead 'for good service in Gascony'. It is interesting to note that out of Alcock's service of only three years, two years accounts are missing.

John remained in Macclesfield manor and in 1363 held a burgage in Wallgate for himself and his 'heirs', which he was forced into mortgaging shortly afterwards. He had a son John Jnr. who seems to have died young not long after his father, neither leaving any significant record in the borough; however, a Roger Alcock (who appears to have been the brother of John Jnr.) was mayor three times (1391-96, 1399-1407, 1417-19) and must have built up something of a family fortune, for his daughter, Alice, inherited the Ridge Hall estate as heiress of the Alcocks. This enabled her to marry well and the estate passed to the Leghs through her marriage.

Alice died childless, so had John of Macclesfield originally been John Alcock he would have made a claim on the estate for recovery of dower. Also there is no alias, or 'known as' in any of the references connected with the two, which was usual. The John Alcock ordained priest in 1378 and sponsored by the Holy Sepulchre at Warwick confirms the Midland connection of this prolific family, and at present it is pure speculation that he was the son of the stock-keeper of Macclesfield.

It seems most unlikely that he would have wanted to change his surname to that of a family who, at that time, was on the same social level as his own. And it hardly seems likely that the surviving members of the Macclesfield family, with whom John of Macclesfield was clearly affiliated, would have welcomed such a change of name, for it would clearly be destined to create confusion under the circumstances.

Also, had the priest John Alcock subsequently changed his name after ordination, surely it would have been in everyone's interest to have made it clear on legal documents.

One of the King's Clerks

The first trace of John of Macclesfield is in the year 1384 when, at the age of 33 to 34 years he is described as one of the 'king's clerks who write at the king's privy seal'. How long he had been there is not known, but he was rewarded with a grant of 100 shillings per annum from March 1385, and the indications are that London was his base of operations from this time on.

If he had been employed previously in the Cheshire administration then it seems likely that he had come to the attention of Sir Hugh Segrave. Sir Hugh, at the insistence of Edward III's wife, Queen Philippa, was keeper of Burstwick castle and the forests of Kingswood and Filwood in Gloucestershire.

When John of Macclesfield was about 22 years old Sir Hugh became steward of the Black Prince's lands in Cheshire, a post which he held for 4 years until the prince's death in 1376. Sir Hugh was also one of the five executors of the Prince's will and during the following year of 1377 became a councillor to the young King, Richard II.

Promotion continued and Sir Hugh became Keeper of the Great Seal on 16th July 1380,

Cows in the fields above Macclesfield where the cows belonging to the Black Prince once pastured and, according to his instructions, were provided with 'cow-houses'.

BOLINGBROKE

WARWICK

GLOUCESTER

ARUNDEL

MOWBRAY

Seals representing the authority of each of the lords appellant. This group was sanctioned by parliament to restrict Richard II's personal power during his minority.

by which all documents were authenticated, including those already bearing the privy (i.e. private) seal of the monarch. He was granted the income from several manors and held the post of treasurer of England from 1381 until his death in 1386. He again had custody of the Great Seal for a few weeks during 1382.

So here was an extremely influential man who would certainly have known John of Macclesfield, and because of the connection with the royal lands was possibly the means by which John was transferred from Cheshire to London.

There were four clerks in the Privy Seal Office and several who copied out documents, but it it likely that John was one of the former. He would be entitled to board and lodgings at a hospice and also clothes (? uniform) all provided by the king. In order to augment their finances the clerks were legitimately entitled to be 'self-employed', and this took many forms e.g. when a royal property became vacant they could advise an interested party who wanted to take up the lease, and consequently receive a fee. Many transactions appeared to work on a sort of commission basis (similar to that relating to salesmen today), whilst others, such as writing letters or preparing legal documents for people in general, would be charged accordingly. And as they accrued more money, the clerks became lenders, which proved extremely lucrative, for if it was a loan on property which the mortagee could not repay, the clerk could legally seize the property through action in a law court.

Macclesfield was later accused of persuading one of his borrowers that it did not matter if the money was not paid on time, saying that he would allow the mortgagee a few extra days, but in the meantime took possession of the property. When the man objected he was put in the king's prison for a spell and decided not to pursue his case further, claiming Macclesfield had friends in 'high places'. It is difficult to judge whether or not Macclesfield was unfairly accused; but even if the mortgagee, desperate to regain his property, had stretched the truth, he must have thought there was a chance of being believed, which suggests that Macclesfield was good at 'smooth-talking'.

Circumstantial evidence suggests that he was involved with the dower lands of the queen, and his handling of matters on behalf of whoever was 'Lady of the Manor of Macclesfield' appears to have stood him in good stead.

Whilst Segrave was treasurer, Michael de la Pole was chancellor (the two posts became one under Elizabeth I), and it is interesting to note that the latter was the son of an extremely wealthy wool merchant of Hull who had made considerable loans to Edward III (Richard II's grandfather) and had been adequately compensated, enabling the family to enjoy a higher social status. Son Michael, having had experience of his father's business, was well suited for high office and was created Earl of Suffolk in 1385.

This seems to have been the hallmark of Richard II's reign; his intelligence and common sense told him that those who were successful in business and had proved loyal and competent during his minority, were capable of high office in the financial administration of his government. His generosity was lavish, feeling they had earned their rewards, but cynics would say he was buying their loyalty.

Richard had reckoned without his royal relatives who saw the family wealth disseminating amongst the lower classes, and decided the time for action had arrived. The ideal regent was the Duke of Lancaster, John of Gaunt, the fourth son of Edward III and therefore Richard's uncle, but the other nobles were unnecessarily fearful of his ambitions and formed a group of councillors known as the Appellants to control Richard's powers and finances.

Two parliaments followed, one in 1386 during which Suffolk was impeached, and one in February 1388 when he was, with others, convicted as a traitor but managed to escape abroad; Richard's old friend and tutor, his faithful servant Sir Simon Burley was executed, despite Queen Anne begging on her knees for his life. Richard never forgave the Appellants for the way in which his wife was spurned.

Parliament seemed determined to sweep away Richard's personnel and it must have been an extremely worrying time for John of Macclesfield. He was obviously learning well the politics of the situation, for he did survive.

One important appointment was that of Robert de Vere, Earl of Oxford (Richard's dearest friend apart from Burley) as justiciar of Cheshire in September 1387, and with Macclesfield's knowledge of the Cheshire finances there is little doubt that he was of good use to de Vere.

Shortly after Richard had seized personal power in May 1389, John of Macclesfield, then aged 40 years, seems to have realised self-preservation was not only essential but a very necessary part of the game.

Detail from Richard II's coronation. His uncle, John of Gaunt is seated on his left wearing an ermine hat.

The Queen Mother

Before continuing the story of Richard II's clerk and secretary, John of Macclesfield, for this month only he has been 'usurped' by a member of our present royal family, the Queen Mother. Why?

One good reason is, of course, because it just happens to be Her Majesty's 100th birthday today, but that you all know; the other, not quite so well-known, is her family's connection with Macclesfield.

Some years ago a Congleton historian, James Blundell, was approached by a lady called Vere Hodgson who felt her family had associations with that town and had been 'rather important'. What unfolded was a fascinating story which later saved me a good deal of time and considerably augmented my research (I was already well and truly involved with tracking down the Roe family for my forthcoming book about Charles Roe and the silk industry of Macclesfield etc.). It also provided me with the opportunity to 'dig deeper' into the lives of an exceptional group of people, and reveal the significant effect each had on the history of Macclesfield from the mid-18th century. Here in brief only are a few of the relevant details.

A delightful photo of the Queen Mother taken by Colin Edwards in October 1997, appropriately as she was leaving St. Paul's cathedral.

After Charles Roe had built the first silk mill complex in Macclesfield, completed in 1748, and the third only in England after Derby (1717) and Stockport(1740), he turned his attention to copper. He had been a general merchant for some time and, inspired by Thomas Patten's copper smelters in Warrington, decided to put all his resources into the revival of this important industry.

By 1758, with a smelter established on Macclesfield Common, he had to ensure a constant and adequate supply of raw materials; copper smelting was an expensive business. A good coal supply was imperative to attain the high temperatures required for the different processes, but the nearby seams on the Common were insufficient and Charles had to look elsewhere for supplementary supplies.

Circumstantial evidence suggests that the important Macclesfield lawyer, John Stafford, town clerk and clerk of the Manor and Forest of Macclesfield on behalf of the Earl of Derby, was the catalyst in what would become a very successful and lifelong partnership between Charles Roe and a character called Brian Hodgson. The latter was able to supply a great quantity of coal from his investments in, and development of, the Disley colliery near Lyme Hall.

Brian Hodgson's father-in-law had been landlord of 'The George' at Stamford, a famous hostelry on the Great North Road leading from London to York; an important route for traders and pilgrims. After his death in 1740 the business was continued by Brian Hodgson for ten years when, together with his wife and nine children, he became tenant of another famous inn, Buxton Hall (now The Old Hall) owned by the Duke of Devonshire. His investments included, not only land at Disley and around Buxton, but also speculations in the lead and copper mining industry of Derbyshire and Staffordshire; and he was a fanatical horse breeder.

By the mid-1760s he had relinquished his tenancy of Buxton Hall in favour of one of his sons, another Brian, and moved to Ashbourne, close by the Duke of Devonshire's copper mine at Ecton Hill from which ore was purchased by Roe. However, his first son, Robert, who like William Roe succeeded to his own father's position in the copper company, is the one relevant to this story.

Both he and William acquired a considerable knowledge of mining, but whereas William also became expert in copper smelting at Toxteth Park, Liverpool, Robert's expertise lay in the production of copper sheets, many hundreds of which were used by the British Navy in the sheathing of ships.

Robert, originally resident in Macclesfield until at least 1767, moved 8 miles south to Daisybank, Congleton and took over supervision of the rolling mills etc. at Havannah in the parish of Eaton.

After many vicissitudes created by the Napoleonic Wars, Robert died in 1808 at St. Alban's, having been mayor of Congleton in 1789 and 1803 and tenant of Moody Hall for a period.

Robert's son, Rev. Robert, became Dean of Carlisle and Rector of St. George's, Hanover Square, London; Rev. Robert's granddaughter, Francis Dora Smith married Claude Lyon-Bowes (13th Earl of Strathmore) in 1853 at Bexley, Kent. The family name was changed to Bowes-Lyon and their granddaughter, christened Lady Elizabeth Angela Marguerite Bowes-Lyon has always been affectionately known as 'The Queen Mum' since her daughter's coronation.

The families were also linked through inter-marriage with the Porteus family, which means that the Queen Mother is distantly related to George Washington, first president of the United States.

Robert Hodgson's wife was Mildred Porteus, whose uncle Dr. Beilby Porteus married Robert's sister, Margaret (the joys of 18th century genealogy!). As Bishop of Chester, Beilby consecrated Charles Roe's New Church, now Christ Church, on 16th November 1779. He subsequently became Bishop of London and was so highly regarded by George III, that after the king's remarkable recovery from his first bout of illness in February 1789, at his 'express command' Beilby preached in St. Paul's Cathedral on the following 23rd April, 'the day of public thanksgiving for His Majesty's recovery'.

We can assume Robert Hodgson was present, but he could never have imagined that almost 211 years later his great granddaughter's granddaughter would also enjoy her own thanksgiving service in St. Paul's for her remarkable life of 100 years. It must be said that many of the Hodgsons too enjoyed longevity; nevertheless they would certainly be proud of the Queen Mother's performance.

Winter at Havannah with the weir built by Roe & Co. clearly visible. Here in the latter half of the 18th century rolling mills produced copper plates used for sheathing naval ships etc. The director of these works, and one of the Roe & Co. partners, was Robert Hodgson from whom the Queen Mother is directly descended.

John de Macclesfield Part II
including Richard II, Dick Whittington
and Bosley manor

With John of Macclesfield's arrival 'on stage' in London, it is time to look at his known career and his sudden obsession to strengthen his ties with Macclesfield town.

After King Richard II had seized personal power in May 1389, by insisting he had 'come of age', the intrigues persisted, and although John of Gaunt remained faithful to the young king, his military duties took him to the Continent conveniently out of harm's way.

Richard, as with previous monarchs, could have continued to use his privy seal, but he began to use his own secret or signet seal, particularly after his mother's death in 1385; it was much smaller than the others and was later set into his finger ring, thus creating a signet ring.

This was probably not an act of defiance so much as a more convenient way of doing things, and a feeling that on reaching the age of 18 he was competent enough to take some decisions on his own, epitomised by the use of his own personal seal. However, after the tragic interference of the Appellants, the signet and its keeper (the secretary) were withdrawn for a

period, and it is important to realise that about this time the Privy Seal Office was moved from the king's court to Westminster, no doubt as a further step in curtailing the king's personal power.

On 9th March 1390 the chancellor restored the signet to the king and immediately Macclesfield appears as a clerk to the signet, the inference being that the clerk (or clerks) would always be with the king and not at Westminster. (The keeper of the signet was Edmund Stafford who would hold the office till 1396).

Richard now favoured his clerk with several grants and appears to have had total trust in him, even allowing Macclesfield to sign a signet letter on 14th February, 1390, before the signet was restored. Perhaps this had been contrived to 'test the water' so that if, parliament objected, Richard could always argue it was his clerk's signature not his that was on the document.

Macclesfield evidently continued to prove

The Bank of England late 18th century. On the extreme right can be seen the tower of St. Bartholomew's church leading round to Pig Street (now Old Broad St.) where St. Anthony's pigs were allowed to run. The hospice was on the opposite side from the church and had become the site of 'The French Church' by this period .

his worth, for Richard petitioned the Pope to allow him the canonries of York, Lichfield and Salisbury, referring to him as his secretary. The term 'secretary' has been much debated by historians and appears to have attracted different connotations at various times. But although Macclesfield does not seem to have gained the importance of subsequent secretaries, yet he was held in high regard by the king who made great efforts to reward him; the most important grant was that of the wardenship of St. Anthony's hospital in the City of London, which he received whilst still in the Privy Seal Office.

St. Anthony's was a satellite of a French establishment; there were many in England at that time but during the wars with France they were occasionally confiscated by the Crown and then returned later. One such confiscation was in 1377 during the first year of Richard II's reign. St. Anthony's, a very wealthy hospice, was then leased to Michael de la Pole for only 20 marks a year – two years later its value was about 400 marks a year!

In the autumn of 1389 John of Macclesfield became warden and it was specified as a gift from the king 'in default of the religious', which again seems to imply that Macclesfield was not in Holy Orders. This is also emphasised by the fact that although the Pope in Rome initially granted Richard's request for Macclesfield to have the canonries of York, Lichfield and Salisbury, yet it was rescinded. This was the time of the Great Schism when there was also a Pope in Avignon, France, supported by some continental rulers – but not the English or Holy Roman Emperor – so both Popes claimed St. Anthony's. The Church had recovered from the effects of the plague almost two generations earlier, so presumably there was no excuse for the appointment of lay members to such posts when once more there were sufficient numbers of ordained priests.

Even the grant of St. Anthony's was not without its difficulties. Officially, as it was run under the Rule of St. Augustine, Macclesfield should have been a member, but he refused the Pope's command. The Pope did not want to offend Richard II; nevertheless Macclesfield lost the post for a while but regained it when the 'technicalities' had been overcome!

Individually Augustinians were not allowed to own property and it is evident that Macclesfield had already decided (presumably with encouragement from Adam de Kyngeslegh,

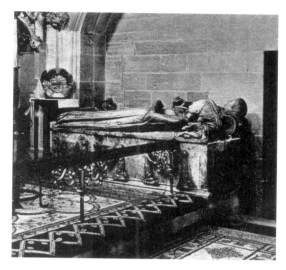

Savage family tombs in Macclesfield Parish Church of the late 15th century. A family with whom John of Macclesfield became closely associated towards the end of the 14th century.

his old associate in Cheshire) to build himself a fine mansion; this he could not do if he entered the Order.

Another important connection was the wealthy mercantile family of Savage from just over the Derbyshire border, but by then established at Runcorn, Cheshire. At that period Runcorn was a very important port on the Mersey, and the trade with N. Ireland particularly Belfast, was considerable.

In 1336 Edward III had assigned the properties and revenues of St. Anthony's to a John Savage (said to be a secular priest) although at one stage it was returned to the French mother house; Savage, however, was left in charge for the three years 1363, 66 & 67 when the then warden visited France. Macclesfield would soon become closely associated with the family and possibly was already.

During 1391 he began to acquire plots of land in what is today the Backwallgate area of Macclesfield town centre, and by July 1393 there was a house on the site, because he was pardoned by Queen Anne, Lady of the Manor and Forest, for taking oak trees without prior permission and using them for building purposes.

Macclesfield wanted security. He must have been aware of the rivalries taking place behind the scenes and somewhere away from London was a shrewd move. Also if he was responsible for the dower lands, his visits to the area would make it a logical proposition to have a residence here, particularly as the Macclesfield family had been so well-known. And if, as suspected, he traded in wool, the business and contacts were already flourishing in the area. Macclesfield town was also ideally situated for travelling in all directions throughout England and beyond.

Richard II

Whilst John of Macclesfield's grand residence was being built in Macclesfield Manor during the years 1391-93 all sorts of intrigues were afoot.

Firstly, and possibly before John began to acquire his plots of land, during 1391 there was a 'mysterious uprising in Cheshire' which some said Richard II had secretly encouraged. It arose from the appointment of the Duke of Gloucester as justiciar of Chester and N. Wales during Richard's minority. Richard was compelled to sanction a life grant of Chester to Gloucester in 1389 much to the chagrin of Cheshire men. When Richard demanded 3000 marks in 1390 for renewing their liberties, only 1000 marks were collected, and the attempts of 1391 to collect the remainder were 'resisted by force'.

It can be no coincidence that John de Macclesfield appeared in the county at this time and began to build his 'stronghold'; within a few months he had become secretary to the king.

Richard knew that there was no greater loyalty to be found anywhere than in Cheshire. When struggling to gain personal power from the Appellants he had initially appointed his dearest friend and confidant, de Vere as Duke of Ireland in October 1386, and within the year made him justiciar of Chester (8th September 1387) adding N. Wales two months later. During this critical period de Vere raised an army in Cheshire, including its famous archers, and marched south in support of Richard, but was defeated (though many claimed he deserted the army at the first sign of real trouble) at Radcot Bridge and fled to the Continent. There were skirmishes, but most of his followers quickly 'melted' into the countryside, making their way home as best they could.

Richard would be anxious to keep the loyalty of these Cheshire men, particularly as Cheshire remained the imperative keystone in keeping the peace in Wales, Ireland and on occasion Scotland. There is little doubt that John de M.'s mission in the county was to reconnoitre, en-

sure support was forthcoming and report to the king. At the same time he appears to have taken it upon himself to establish a satellite office which he conveniently sited in Macclesfield Manor, an action which he must have considered Richard would later condone. This would account for the fact that he took oak trees from the forest without first obtaining Queen Anne's permission, certain of the king's approval and therefore hers, but did have to obtain her subsequent pardon as a legality.

If the tide did turn against Richard then John de M. could conveniently withdraw to Macclesfield and, being away from the centres of power such as Chester and London, had a chance to ride out any storms ahead. He was obviously not alone in this and had powerful local allies such as Adam de Kyngeslegh. However, during 1392, when things had settled down in Cheshire, a more urgent task had to be undertaken. Richard sent John de M. to Rome on a diplomatic mission to the Pope, so someone must have been left in charge of his building programme in Macclesfield.

Because of the schism many problems had arisen. In 1389 Urban VI had died and Boniface IX became Pope in Rome and 'expressed a desire to end the schism'. The greatest problem was how the Italian pope could manage to keep

Robert de Vere justiciar of Chester 1387. Exiled in France he was gored by a boar whilst out hunting in 1392 and died from his wounds.

the enormous church mechanism functioning when only half his revenues could be collected. At that time in England the Appellants, to strengthen their powers and finances, took steps to limit the pope's powers, but the English clergy supported the pope.

By 1391 all sorts of schemes were being devised throughout Europe, with the French intent on restoring their Pope Clement to Rome from Avignon. The view of the English parliament differed at times from that of Richard II and his uncle, John of Gaunt, but in 1392 negotiations for peace with France were underway, yet with the involvement of the Duke of Gloucester progress ground to a halt.

Richard was an extremely religious man and has been much misunderstood by many historians. He was a monarch ahead of his time, a man of peace, of great intelligence and culture, and never interested in tournaments or waging wars, but he did realise that a show of strength was necessary to keep the peace. He was also anxious to become Holy Roman Emperor like his father-in-law before him, and he was a Dominican of the Third Order (i.e. lay Order,) a fact which is regularly overlooked but which is a great indicator to his character.

Richard was unfortunately surrounded by men who loved jousting, showing off their physical abilities and who saw in Richard weaknesses judged from their own standards of behaviour. Richard was 'all forgiving' and rewarded people well for their service and loyalty; the Appellants construed this as a form of bribery. Anxious to demonstrate his support for the Pope in Rome and, it would seem, to allow John de M. to state his case for receiving the canonries of York, Lichfield and Salisbury, Richard sent John to Rome granting him letters of protection on 26th January, 14th & 28th February 1292 to cover his long arduous journey.

John must have been successful, for in May the Pope granted him the three canonries, yet once more fate took a hand and the cardinals, despairing of Boniface's demands for revenues, forced him to leave Rome later that year, but he was able to return in December 1393. John de M.'s efforts on his own behalf proved to be in vain, for the Pope rescinded the grant of the three canonries.

Once again this does seem to indicate that John de M. was not in Holy Orders, because of the constant difficulties he had in obtaining the various ecclesiastical benefits which Richard II

The Vatican, Rome today but not as John of Macclesfield would have seen it. The Vatican at that time was on the site, but was a basilica built by Constantine which, though deteriorating, became the papal residence in 1377. It was Julius II (1503-1513) who began the work of building the new basilica, completed 176 years later.

was anxious to bestow on him. Many other government clerks who were ordained obtained far more preferences than John de M., some of them acquiring vast estates.

Whilst John was travelling on the Continent Richard attended several councils and began to gain respect for his views and judgements, but unfortunately fell out with the mayor and aldermen of London who refused him a loan. They were arrested, a fine imposed and a personal gift extracted, but after mediation from Queen Anne concordant relations were restored, however the City would not forget these actions.

During 1394 many important people died, amongst them Queen Anne on 7th June. Richard was devastated; this was the turning point, not only for him but also England and John de M.

Christmas

The Chronicler Thomas Walsingham, a Benedictine monk of St. Alban's Abbey, describes how on Christmas Day 1391 a dolphin leapt its way up river from the Thames Estuary to London Bridge. It was eventually caught by a group of citizens and taken into London, having considered it to be 'an interesting spectacle for the people, since it was easily ten feet long'.

Whether or not John de Macclesfield was able to see the dolphin for himself, may never be known, but it does seem likely that he had left Cheshire and returned south in preparation for his journey to Rome and to spend Christmas with the Ricardian court.

Although Richard II's itinerary is sometimes difficult to unravel, yet he regularly appears to have preferred touring in the south of England during the autumn seasons, and then conveniently spending Christmas and the New Year at one of his country palaces outside London. For instance, in 1388 and again in 1392 he celebrated Christmas at Eltham, whilst in 1395 he was at Kennington Manor.

Richard was a connoisseur, and the court had become a centre of cultural and artistic excellence, so one can well imagine the magnificence of the Christmas and New Year celebrations whilst still respecting their deeply religious significance. It is interesting to note that the first reference to Geoffrey Chaucer was in his grand-father, Edward III's court at Christmas 1357 when Chaucer, as a young boy, was page to the Countess of Ulster, Edward III's daughter-in-law.

A cookery book still exists which contains 196 recipes compiled by Richard's master cook, and there is no doubt that John de Macclesfield would have been able to enjoy many of the royal dishes. Spices were very much in evidence, particularly pepper (both 'whole' and powdered) and ginger; also cinnamon, cardamom, nutmeg and saffron. Sugar was widely used, either 'white' or clarified with wine, but the speciality was 'sugar of Cyprus'. (Having returned from Cyprus bearing a couple of bottles of Commandaria St. John, a rich desert wine similar to Madeira and still produced with the same recipe as that used at the time of the Crusades, I can well imagine the delicious taste of sugar clarified with this particular wine!).

There appears to have been three courses to a meal; firstly the potage – a favourite was venison broth; next the main course e.g. oysters cooked in Greek wine or minced flesh of pheas-

Backwallgate today: the trees on the left of the photo represent the area originally taken up by part of John de Macclesfield's 'castle'. The view point is from what would have been part of his lower field where, one suspects, many of Richard's entourage would have set up camp because of the proximity of the Town's Well (then just to the right of the photo). However, it would have been extremely cold because the visit took place early in the year.

ant also cooked in Greek wine but flavoured with cinnamon, cloves and ginger to which 2lbs. of sugar was added. Sometimes rice was served with the main course. Often olive oil was used instead of butter, and 'Lumbard Mustard' from Italy as a condiment.

Finally came the third course which was a solitee and could be either savoury (made with meat paste) or sweet, such as mulberries with honey. This final course appears to have been the opportunity to provide an elaborate display of different colours, designs and shapes, and the whole meal was accompanied by either plenty of Rhenish wine or that from La Rochelle, whilst another favourite was a strong white wine from Italy called 'Vernage'.

Surprisingly meat does not seem to have been served whole at the table in the Ricardian court, there are no references to haunches of venison or roasted ox for example; and from the recipes provided the suggestion is that the men and women of the court circle mostly ate with spoons and not their hands.

One of Richard's 'fetishes' was the use of a handkerchief which, because of the beautiful and elaborate court dress, possibly started life as a table napkin; however, despite his efforts he was not very successful in promoting its usage.

The King's penultimate Christmas was spent at Lichfield before he travelled into Cheshire as the guest of John de Macclesfield early in 1399. John had completed the crenellation and fortification of his residence in stone the previous year, and must have considered it 'fit for a king', but the problem would have been where to accommodate the considerable entourage. At this period Richard's personal bodyguard was made up of 300-400 Cheshire archers, and the royal household included minstrels, artists and artificers, so it would have been quite an event for the then small borough to play host to such a gathering.

There seems little doubt that Richard's master cook would have been part of the complement, and whereas Richard's father, the Black Prince, had ordered six roe deer to be sent from Macclesfield Forest some years earlier for a banquet in Chester, on this occasion the main course was fresh trout.

Richard would certainly have attended Mass at the parochial chapel (now the parish church of St. Michael's) with John de Macclesfield and one wonders if the superb Wilton Diptych was unpacked for the service. This beautiful port-

From ancient times the dolphin has been a creature of myths and legends, adorning various works of art and more utilitarian objects such as this 18th century Delft tile. Unusually it does not depict a boy riding the dolphin, but a cherub – quite appropriate when considering Richard II's use of angels on his many emblems. Not surprisingly John de Macclesfield 'borrowed' an angel for his own seal.

able altar piece, painted on both sides, features Richard wearing a broom-pod collar and kneeling before St. Mary the Virgin and the infant Christ. A group of angels are also wearing the broom-pod collars (in addition to Richard's white hart badges) which were derived from French livery after the device had been presented to the young king by Charles VI of France in 1396: the diptych therefore cannot predate the gesture.

By the time of Richard's visit to the borough John de Macclesfield was Keeper of the Great Wardrobe, an important post as he was responsible for thousands of pounds worth of equipment etc. in what was effectively the royal warehouse.

Dick Whittington

Incredible as it seems John would have known the real Dick Whittington. Although the early lives of both are somewhat shrouded in mystery, it is believed that Richard Whittington was born in Gloucestershire and arrived in London about 1371.

The River Thames via Lechlade carried a considerable amount of trade between the two areas, so young Richard was apprenticed to a London Mercer, Sir Ivo Fitzwayn, who no doubt did business with his father. The Mercers Company (which received its charter in 1393) was represented in Flanders by the Merchant Adventurers.

Whittington must have worked hard, but how the cat came into the story is unknown. Yet myths and legends have a way of developing from true facts, and the story, which first appeared in print in 1605, does have a ring of truth to it. The Mercers dealt in high quality goods which were easily destroyed by vermin, especially the expensive silks and velvets, and it has been proved on many occasions that the only way to rid a place of rats and other vermin is by using cats, especially on board ship. So perhaps Whittington was fortunate to have a

Sir Richard Whittington: portrait engraved by Renold Elstacke early 17th century, but with no guarantee it is an authentic likeness. The original depicts Whittington's right hand resting on a skull but popular demand forced Elstacke to change the emblem to a cat.

cat which was a superb mouser which kept a cargo of his master's goods from being attacked and eaten. He did marry Sir Ivo's daughter, Alice, which suggests he made his fortune and was able to provide an appropriate sum for the marriage settlement.

Having become an alderman, Whittington was appointed Mayor of London in June 1397 by Richard II on the death of Adam Bamme, and in October was elected for the following year; he also became master of the Mercers Company. He served as Mayor of London on two further occasions, but these were in the reigns of Henry IV in 1406-7 and Henry V in 1419-20.

He was given overall responsibility for Henry V's continuation of the great building work on the nave of Westminster Abbey, and himself built two libraries, one for the Guildhall. Out of the bequests in his will for charitable purposes (he was a widower with no children), his concern for the dreadful state of Newgate prison saw a new prison built, and his burial took place at St. Michael (College Hill), a church which he had rebuilt during his lifetime. Unfortunately his grave and church were destroyed by the Great Fire together with Newgate prison, but rebuilding did occur and on the latter was placed a sculpture of a man with a cat at his feet; hence the presumption that it was a representation of Dick Whittington and his cat.

Whittington also appears to have had the lease for Leadenhall Market, which was taken over by London Corporation in 1411, and he was at one time collector of customs for the port of London.

Merchants

Another important London merchant, with whom John de Macclesfield did business, was Gilbert Maghfeld. He first appears as an agent in the great Hanseatic port of Danzig in 1367 (today Gdansk in Poland but with early Germanic connections) and then established himself in Billingsgate, London. The name is intruiging, for Maghfeld would be the German equivalent of Macclesfield, and Gilbert was certainly a Christian name in the Macclesfield family. Also it was business practice to use family members as much as possible, so it is not beyond the bounds of probability that the two were closely related.

In the early 1380s Maghfeld and three others operated the customs patrols from Berwick-on-Tweed to Winchelsea and would have worked with Chaucer, who was for a time controller of customs. It is interesting to note that so important was the trade with German merchants, they were granted their own community area and quay on the north bank of the Thames together with exemption from customs duties.

In 1394 Maghfeld advanced £50 and, together with the clerk of the navy and a sergeant-at-arms, equipped three ships for Richard II's Irish expedition which included artillery etc. He was a general wholesaler dealing in goods which included building supplies (lead, stones, Prussian wainscot, iron and copper) and also spices, silk, wool, furs; even fish and pearls! His accounts confirm that he was able to provide loans to London Corporation and to many earls, bishops and abbots, amongst many.

John de Macclesfield, after his gift of the wardenship of St. Anthony's hospital in 1389, began a programme of repairs and maintenance between the summers of 1390-91. Considerable amounts of wainscot were purchased from Maghfeld and the pavement outside was relaid

Collage: Whittington's cat – a popular pantomime character. Among the most notable performances is that on Boxing Day 1814 at Covent Garden (London was celebrating Napoleon's exile on Elba!) called 'Harlequin Whittington' or 'The Lord Mayor of London' (N.B. it was plain mayor at the time of Whittington – only Lord Mayor later). The famous clown Grimaldi played 'Mistress Cecily Suet'. In 1884 at the Alexandra Theatre, Walsall; there was a burlesque entitled 'Dick Whittington and his CATastrophe'. But the Queen's Theatre, Battersea in 1894 was nearer to producing the modern version – a pantomime 'Dick Whittington and his cat'.

– the cost also included the workman's lunches, presumably also provided by Maghfeld (which certainly conjures up a sort of 'meals on wheels' idea).

John de Macclesfield also persuaded Maghfeld to invest in some of his property deals, but unfortunately by 1397 the merchant was bankrupt, largely due to vast sums of money owed by a named but otherwise unknown customer (could this have been on behalf of the king?) – it made no difference to Maghfeld, his chattels were seized and he died shortly afterwards.

With Maghfeld's demise Richard Whittington appears to have come to the fore and advanced enormous sums to Richard II; however, he did head the list of city merchants forced to make contributions to Richard in 1394. But with Richard's capture and forfeiture of the crown, Whittington was called to Henry IV's council in December 1399 when all royal debts were repaid and he became financier to the new king.

At the beginning of his second term of mayor in 1406 Whittington was fortunate in capturing an impostor posing as Richard II, which finally put an end to rumours of the young king's survival. He made considerable loans to Henry V, was knighted by him (as stated in a modern history article, although Victorian historians considered he had never been knighted) and finally died in 1423, the year after John de Macclesfield. The contrast could not have been greater; Richard died an extremely wealthy but childless, man; John left little, having given up his hard won gains for the sake of his several illegitimate children's inheritances.

New Year Customs

For many the holly with its bright red berries, and the mistletoe with its white, are very much part of the Christmas trappings. Yet in the British Isles the mistletoe in ancient times was associated with the New Year.

This evergreen plant is a parasite growing mostly on apple trees but can also be found on pear, willow, hawthorn and poplar, yet very rarely on oak. It is propagated by the mistle-thrush (a bird slightly larger than the song-thrush but with a less interesting call) which eats the berries and then wipes its beak against the bark of a tree. The seed germinates, growing a root which penetrates the bark of the tree, allowing the mistletoe to 'feed' off its host.

For centuries it was considered to have magical and medicinal properties and because of this became revered by the Druids, especially if found growing on an oak, the tree which they considered sacred. Having found the prize, one of the Druids dressed in a white robe would climb the tree and carefully cut down the bunches with a golden knife.

This elaborate ceremony was, however, only performed at the beginning of the year when the moon was at a particular stage of its monthly cycle, for then the Druids were obliged to have visions telling them when to search for the elusive evergreen. If the visions were long in coming, or the mistletoe was dropped and fell to the ground, a 'national' calamity was considered inevitable.

There is a tradition that the Druids had a considerable relgious centre on the site of what is now the parish church of Ashbourne in Derbyshire, and were active in the Whetton area. Because of the extent of the early forest around Macclesfield they must surely have frequented this area also. It is said that their main religious centre, from which the responsibilty for teaching and governing this region came, was actually on Anglesey.

With the coming of Christianity the mistletoe was incorporated into the decorations of the Festive Season. In later centuries it was often hung in farmhouse kitchens, and in England a custom arose whereby kissing under the mistletoe was considered a sure way of leading to marriage (perhaps a convenient way of ensuring that the man found himself a good cook for a wife!). When this tradition began is difficult to deduce, but a Victorian engraving depicts a young man stealing a kiss from a pretty girl whilst holding a bunch of mistletoe over her head. In the background two characters are gathering bunches of mistletoe from what appears to be an oak tree, but all are dressed in 17th century costumes.

Some of the earliest references to mistletoe are from around the end of the first millenium, and as the borough of Macclesfield came into being in the 13th century and freemen began to establish their gardens, there can be no doubt that with the planting of apple and pear trees in the borough, a crop of mistletoe would be inevitable, and also in the surrounding forest area with the hawthorn prevelant.

Victorian engraving as mentioned in the text.

The Kynges Legh Affair

By the end of the 14th century John de Macclesfield had acquired a burgage with an orchard on Chestergate, and although it was let, he ensured that he was allowed the fruit from the trees growing in the orchard. There was also an orchard adjacent to the western side of Jordangate which seems to have covered a fairly substantial area stretching down towards the River Bollin (the latter name had been adopted by this period). This too had originally been owned by the Macclesfield family at an earlier period.

With the association of mistletoe and the hope of marriage, it is appropriate to consider John de Macclesfield's intruiging relationship with Katherine de Kyngeslegh, a relationship which seems to have begun in earnest about 1394-95. John had been to Rome in 1392, was involved in London affairs in 1393 (i.e. St. Giles hospital and the preparations for Richard II's Irish campaign) and accompanied the King to Ireland in 1394. On his return his ties with Cheshire were strengthened, firstly by association with John Savage and his wife Maude.

Savage has gained the advowson of Barrow (now Great Barrow just to the north of Tarvin and 4 miles from Chester) by a lawsuit, and presented John de Macclesfield with the rectorship in 1396.

By the time of the fortification of John's residence in Macclesfield (1398) Katherine must have also been living there, as by 1402 she had presented him with two sons, John Jnr. and William. During 1396 her father and mother, Adam and Ellen de Kyngeslegh had settled land and rents on John, almost in the way of a marriage settlement, and that year John went to great lengths to acquire title to the extremely lucrative Bosley Manor, see pp186-187.

By 1396 Adam had been in Cheshire at least 35 years which suggests he must have been in his mid to late 50s at this time. Katherine has been considered young, for she did bear John de Macclesfield three more sons and finally a daughter (the latter in 1415), therefore she appears to have been a younger child. There is evidence of a brother John (or cousin) but as her mother's name was Ellen, perhaps she was named after a grandmother. Is it possible Katherine had an elder sister?

No one has considered that John of Macclesfield could have been married earlier. By 1396 he was in his mid-40s and, based on the evidence, a particularly virile man. Perhaps his wife was barren, in a convent or had died, and perhaps she was Katherine's older sister.

This would explain the total trust the Kyngesleghs had in John; the reason why he could not marry Katherine (the Church forbad marriages to a deceased wife's sister); and the trouble with Katherine's 'brother' who would consider 'the dower' his if she was not legally married. Hence his raiding of the Macclesfield household when he confiscated several valuable goods.

Conspiracy

It is almost time to bid farewell to John de Macclesfield having spent most of the millennium year with him (which seemed appropriate as he was one of our earliest 'premier' townsmen to have left a considerable impression). His association with Macclesfield signals the end of an era for the borough i.e. a period of direct royal involvement which had begun little more than a century earlier with the visits of Edward I and his queen, Eleanor of Castile.

From time to time the forest had attracted several members of the royal family and their hunting parties; but all that was about to change.

In 1386 Richard II had rightly declared Roger Mortimer (Earl of March and grandson of his uncle the Duke of Clarence) his heir apparent. Unfortunately young Mortimer was murdered by 'wild' Irishmen, which had forced Richard to undertake his second Irish expedition in the late spring of 1399, shortly after his Macclesfield visit.

Whilst John of Gaunt lived (he was also Duke of Lancaster and the next youngest uncle to Richard after the Duke of Clarence) all was well, but in that fateful year of 1399 he had died on 3rd February. Shortly afterwards Richard, aware of the many intrigues taking place, declared Gaunt's son, Henry Bolingbroke, exiled instead of suffering a ten year banishment, which gave Richard the opportunity legally to confiscate the enormous Lancastrian estates.

Bolingbroke awaited his opportunity and, whilst Richard was engaged in Ireland, attempted to invade England during the summer. Richard hurriedly sailed for Wales where he had organised support which included that of his Cheshire squires and archers, but Bolingbroke, anticipating the move, had rushed to Chester. A rumour of Richard's death was spread in advance, so his expected main army had 'melted away' leaving him with only his loyal supporter the Earl of Salisbury and a few others.

Richard, safe in Conwy Castle could easily have sailed away, as the ships in the harbour offered friendly assistance. Deluded into believing that his safety and position were paramount if certain conditions were met, Richard accepted the word of Bolingbroke's envoys, the Bishop of Arundel and the Earl of Northumberland. The trio set out to meet Bolingbroke but were ambushed en route, and Richard found himself a prisoner in Flint Castle.

The later Lancastrian chroniclers distorted the truth, but the fact remained that Bolingbroke, a widower of 34 years of age, was determined to seize the throne for himself and not for another Mortimer. Richard was taken to London where he was expected to abdicate. The journey was not without incident, near Lichfield an attempt was made to rescue him, some said by Welsh supporters, others by those from Cheshire, but nothing was gained.

At this point the intriguing question is – 'Where was John de Macclesfield?' He must have been in a very vulnerable position and extremely worried, for he had been appointed Keeper of the Great Wardrobe on 26th November 1397 with effect from the following 2nd February. However, although the office of the Great Wardrobe accompanied Richard to Ireland in 1399 (all offices of state were represented in the king's entourage wherever he went) John de Macclesfield remained in England, no doubt in London, but nevertheless he had been busy fortifying and crenellating his Macclesfield residence with stone. Perhaps a warning had been given by his 'friends in high places'.

After imprisonment in the Tower of London, Richard's supposed abdication in favour of Henry was soon accepted (29th September). Surprisingly the Earl of Salisbury was shortly released from prison which suggests that he had perhaps concurred with the statement that Richard had agreed to abdicate whilst at Conwy.

The city of London, long antagonised by Richard, was totally unprepared to help, and with the status quo virtually maintained in the civil service, most of the population, weary of the years of feuding, quietly acquiesed.

However, John de Macclesfield was not reappointed as Keeper of the Great Wardrobe, and was replaced on the first day of Henry IV reign, 30th September 1399. Richard's mysterious death in Pontefract Castle took place early in the following year and John's allegiance to the new king was assured.

In March 1400 Henry, as Earl of Chester, did allow John de Macclesfield a lease of the herbage and pasture of Macclesfield Park which included the park-keeper's house and hempyard (now the site of Harvest Printers Ltd. by the Park Lane roundabout), although there was an upset with John de Kyngeslegh who claimed he held an unexpired lease. Another important grant of August 1402 saw Bosley Manor settled on the Macclesfields, father and sons, and finally, confirmation of the granting of the fortification of the Macclesfield residence was received in 1410.

Bosley was the most extensive and lucrative manor in Cheshire and (by coincidence) had been developed by the Earls of Salisbury (de Montagu family) for which they had paid a considerable fine to Richard II's father, the Black Prince. In 1401 John de Macclesfield paid the dowager Countess of Salisbury for the title, which extended his holdings in the area as he had already leased the adjacent area of Wincle in the previous year. Wincle Grange belonged

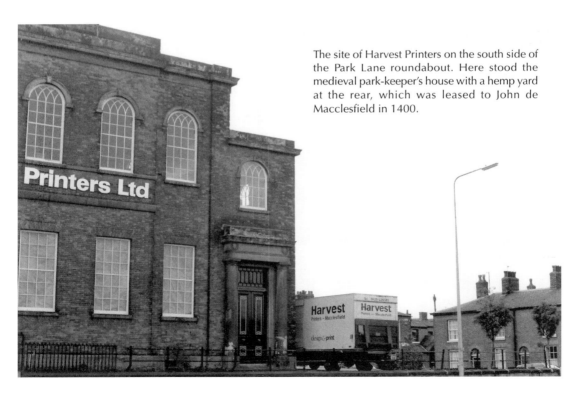

The site of Harvest Printers on the south side of the Park Lane roundabout. Here stood the medieval park-keeper's house with a hemp yard at the rear, which was leased to John de Macclesfield in 1400.

An Old Man

At the time of Henry IV's death John de Macclesfield was about 62-63 years of age. Four years later, on 31st October 1417 he would describe himself as 'sixty six years and more, broken by age and infirmity', afflictions suffered for at least a dozen or so years. He complained of 'weakness' in his back (he was probably suffering from acute arthritis), and on one occasion a pain in his stomach; but he did manage to sire three more sons and finally a daughter between 1407 and 1415!

The daughter was named Maud (de Kyngeslegh not Macclesfield); one would have expected her to be called Katherine after her mother, or Ellen after her grandmother. The wife of John Savage was called Maud, so most likely she was godmother to the child. The circumstances do beg the question, was Macclesfield father to these additional, children, particularly Maud? Whatever the true answer, he did accept them as his own, but already, after the births of his first two sons, he had taken steps to provide for his 'dynasty'.

After Richard II's sudden eclipse, John seemed determined to salvage what he could of his career. Although the tide had turned, Henry IV was anxious 'not to rock the boat', so John, amongst many, had been retained as a civil servant in some capacity, despite having been deprived of his position as Keeper of the Great Wardrobe. He now had heirs, and if his eldest son, John Jnr., survived, in order to marry well, property was needed to provide for a substantial marriage settlement.

Feeling more confident and in possession of, what he must have considered was effectively the grand Macclesfield manor house (complementing his leasing of the park lands etc.), he set about consolidating his holdings in and around the Macclesfield area.

During the year 1402, as he prepared for his journey to Rome, he feverishly acquired property in the borough and worked hard to establish his right to the leasing of Bosley manor. He possibly feared that he might not return safely, therefore his heirs were his paramount consideration; it is interesting to note that Katherine would have to wait her turn.

One unfortunate fact was that Bosley manor was under lease from the Crown to the Salisburys, who had then subleased, and as the Earl had been the only supporter left with Richard in Conwy Castle, although pardoned, the prop-

Henry IV son of John of Gaunt. He seized the throne from Richard II and was declared king on 30th September 1399, the day on which John de Macclesfield was replaced as Keeper of the Great Wardrobe.

to the Cistercian Abbey of St. Mary Combermere with permission to pasture 2,000 sheep, so perhaps this is an indication of John's interest in acquiring the vast tracts of land which must have totalled at least 1,000 acres i.e. sheep rearing and the woollen trade.

In April 1402 Henry IV married Joan of Navarre by proxy and John travelled once more to Rome in the hope of obtaining renewal of his wardenship of St. Anthony's hospice from the Pope. He still seems to have been connected with the royal court, but then in 1413 Henry died.

erty could have been seized back into the king's hands. It must be explained that in general seizure of property, although sounding somewhat dramatic, had to be substantiated through the courts, and no one was above the law, not even the king. In other words justice had to be seen to be done, and often it was. John received his grant of Bosley manor in August 1402. But what of Katherine's situation?

Her father had obviously intended her to be safe, secure and well provided for, thus encouraging the relationship with John de Macclesfield, but about this time he seems to have died. Historians have deduced that John de Kyngeslegh was Katherine's brother; he could have been her cousin, but one fact is apparent, he certainly acted in an authoritative manner with regard to the Kyngesleghs' affairs, which suggests he was heir to the estate. On several occasions he acted as trustee for some of Macclesfield's property deals, but he had also become an ardent Lancastrian supporter and was now ready to cause trouble.

Macclesfield suddenly found himself taken up with ecclesiastical problems in London. The government was intent on reforming hospitals (somehow this sounds familiar!) and once more considering the confiscation of alien (i.e. foreign) priories, so Macclesfield now became embroiled in a series of legal battles to retain his lucrative posts as warden of both St. Anthony's and St. Giles-in-the-Fields hospitals in London.

Katherine too was fighting for her rights, but in a more subtle way. She appears to have been a strong, determined woman, who had literally been left 'holding the baby', and realised she was in an extremely vulnerable position. There seems little doubt that she badgered Macclesfield into including her in his property deals, and from 1407 she succeeded; whether or not it was cause or effect, she did produce another son, Thomas, in July 1407.

In many ways one has to feel sorry for Katherine who was very much a victim of circumstance. By 1410 she had given birth to two more sons, Ralph and Nicholas, and was left to run a considerable household, though obviously with local support, particularly from the Legh family.

Peter (Piers) Legh of Lyme, steward of the lordship of Macclesfield, had unfortunately been beheaded in 1399 for his support of Richard II, which must have left much tension in the area and sent out a warning to all others. He

An English traveller dressed in a riding habit, typical of the reign of Richard II. John de Macclefield would have spent many days and weeks in the saddle dressed in a similar outfit.

had acted as trustee with Adam de Kyngeslegh for many of Macclesfield's property deals. His second son, John, through his marriage to the heiress of the Alcocks, had secured Ridge Hall in the marriage settlement, which would pass to Roger, his heir. Thus began a new branch of the family with whom Katherine was particularly associated.

John de Macclesfield, although still a very cultured man, was deteriorating. He had fallen out of favour, so his ambitions at court had no hope of bearing fruition. He was a tired old man who had probably lost much of his charism and charm due to his debilitating illnesses; he was fighting for his very existence.

A delightful Russian painting depicting early 15th century merchants taking horses to be sold. As John de Macclesfield travelled through central Europe on his way to and from Rome, (most likely via the port of Hamburg), he would have met such groups coming from the East.

Katherine must have longed for security and prestige; it is a story repeated throughout history, an older man at the end of his career with unfulfilled ambitions, trying desperately to hold on to a relationship with a younger vibrant woman. And, as is so often the case, that woman being the mother of his heirs. John finally 'capitulated' and in 1413 made an important decision.

* * *

The Final Years

On 9th April 1413 the new king, Henry V, gave notice of a general pardon which could be claimed before 1st August, 'to all evil-doers except those who had committed murder and rape'. This also concerned those who had been formerly employed by Richard II, and John de Macclesfield received his pardon on 13th June. Probably as a consequence he was able to transfer the lease for the extremely lucrative Bosley Manor to Katherine de Kyngeslegh for life, and after her death to his heirs. So Katherine became lady of the manor of Bosley.

Also in that year a marriage was contracted between their eldest son, John Jnr., and Margaret, the daughter of John Savage. They were young children at the time, at which point the marriage would not have been consummated. A large marriage settlement was agreed, with both Savage and Macclesfield contributing several properties, however the marriage seems to have been annulled, for in 1417 both fathers, through court action, recovered their properties. The children subsequently married others.

The whole episode must have been devastating, after all, the Savage family was becoming one of the premier families in Cheshire; in other words the Savages were 'going places', the Macclesfields were not.

The gift of Bosley to Katherine appears to have been, in part, compensation for those properties included in the settlement, for she too had contributed those given by her parents.

John de Macclesfield had tried to appease Katherine in 1406 by acquiring property in Havering atte Bower, Essex for the benefit of their sons, John Jnr. and his brother, William, but initially with a life interest intended for

Typical female dress of the reign of Henry V of the type which would have been worn by Katherine de Kyngeslegh.

upon marriage, she had waited a little longer for the manor of Havering together with Hertford castle. Henry was more than generous by allowing her a substantial increase in dower of about a third, so evidently she also acquired Bosley, because it was Joan who allowed Macclesfield to transfer the Bosley lease to Katherine.

This link between the manors of Bosley and Macclesfield would create great problems during the reign of Edward IV (grandson of Henry V), when Bosley was seized into the king's hands whilst considerable legal arguments ensued as to ownership.

Meanwhile, returning to John de Macclesfield, the year 1417 was proving an eventful one, as he set out for Constance where a council was taking place to try to end the Schism (i.e. the problem of the two popes). In November of that year Martin V would become pope in Rome and retain office until February 1431.

From 1414 Macclesfield had tried in vain to hold onto his wardenships; he had used couriers and trusted colleagues to take gifts in gold and legal documents to papal officials. One, however, had turned the tables and managed to get himself appointed to St. Anthony's in Macclesfield's stead! There was no alternative, Macclesfield set out for Constance with a small entourage.

Having reached Basle he was so ill that the journey was abandoned and once more proctors were used, one of whom was 'a kinsman and close friend', John Fyton, rector of Stockport (family of Gawsworth). He sent valuable gifts comprising embroidered robes, bed drapes and greyhounds with jewelled collars etc. to various people, and finally had his wardenship of St. Anthony's confirmed.

By 1421 Henry V had also honoured Macclesfield's entitlements, but in preparing his will, shortly before his death on 7th April 1422, John de Macclesfield had little left to bequeath, and there was no sentimental token for the mother of his heirs. By preparing a cartulary of deeds in 1416 he had ensured the legality of the transfers of his properties to his illegitimate sons, and also Katherine's independence. Cartularies were usually prepared by monastic houses or those of great families, so it was unusual, though fortunate from our point of view, that he took this step, thus leaving a wealth of fascinating information.

The Macclesfield mansion was lavishly furnished; in a 'raid' of late 1416 John de

Katherine. Unfortunately his attempts failed; yet the episode does indicate that he had probably returned to his old position of looking after the Queen's dower lands. Traditionally certain large estates, amongst them the manor and forest of Macclesfield and Havering atte Bower, were always used in marriage settlements for the benefit of the kings' wives, and Joan of Navarre, duchess of Brittany (a widow who had become the second wife of Henry IV in April 1402 by proxy) was no exception.

However, whilst receiving most of them

A betrothal feast of the period, honouring the bride, Perhaps Katherine de Kyngeslegh was, at last, able to enjoy such a feast upon her betrothal to John Legh of Ridge.

Kyngeslegh managed to carry off a quantity of expensive furniture, bed hangings, embroidered garments, silverware, illuminated manuscripts and jewels. Some or all of these could have been Katherine's family possessions, for she took court action and was supported in judgement by Sir John Stanley.

Her ties with the Legh family were strengthened when she was godmother to John Legh's (of Ridge) child by 'another woman'. When his wife died is not known, but Katherine's affair with him had begun before Macclesfield's death. Her Bosley lease proved its worth, the two were married and John Legh took control of the manor.

A technicality arose whereby, as Katherine was godmother to John Legh's child, the marriage had to be sanctioned by the pope. Martin V sent a mandate to the Bishop of Lichfield on 26th April 1422 allowing them 'to remain in the marriage they had contracted and celebrated before the church'. Perhaps fearing a legal challenge at a later date, another ceremony appears to have taken place on 11th May.

The contract was certainly executed before Macclesfield's death. Where he is buried we shall probably never know, for he left no specific instructions. Katherine died leaving no legitimate children, and of the others it was through son, Ralph, that the line of descent continued.

Jordan

Shortly after arriving in Macclesfield some 34 years ago, I remember being introduced to someone called 'Nellie' (a blonde-haired lady who wore glasses) whose claim to fame was that she had made silk ties destined for King Hussein of Jordan. Recent enquiries have established that her surname was possibly 'Drinkwater', but that she had died some time ago. I cannot even remember which company she had worked for, yet it was one of those snippets of information which had stuck in my mind.

My subsequent researches have, of course, revealed further local connections with that country; one obvious example is the name Jordangate, and the name of the river as Jordan, also known as the Water of 'E', but which today is the river Bollin.

Whether used as a surname or christian name, Jordan appears to have been brought back to Europe by crusaders returning from the Holy Land. It is interesting to note that after Baldwin, Archbishop of Canterbury, had preached from the High Cross in Chester in support of the Fifth Crusade to the Holy Land (1217-21), many joined Ranulf (Randle) Blunderville, Earl of Chester, on his journey to the Holy Land in 1219. He is said to have distinguished himself in Egypt and on his return built Beeston Castle.

One of the earliest Dominican friars and Master General of the Order was Jordan of Saxony, and again there are many local connections with the Dominicans. It was said to be Queen Eleanor's favourite Order, founded by Dominic be Guzman who had been born in her father's Spanish kingdom of Castile. Therefore it was possibly at her insistence that her parochial chapel of Macclesfield (now St. Michael's Parish Church) was consecrated by the Bishop of St. Asaph, a Dominican, and not the Bishop of Lichfield.

Eleanor's forest bailiff, Thomas de Macclesfield, named his eldest son, Jordan, which does not seem to have been a traditional name in the

Graeco-Roman columns adjacent to the Cathedral at Jerash in Jordan. The second one from the left is perpetually in motion! Columns such as these inspired our Georgian ancestors when creating architectural designs, our town hall being a fine example.

family, thus implying it had some important significance.

Having had three holidays cancelled to Israel and Jordan, within the past few years, my desire to see the famous river and the surrounding region became more intense. Suddenly an invitation to visit Jordan came from an American friend (married to a Jordanian) who has had a home in that country for many years. Along with it came a second invitation to take part in an archaeological dig at Petra with ACOR (American Center for Oriental Research), which I soon discovered was a rare privilege allowed to very few.

Needless to say, the opportunity was seized, arrangements made within the month, and I was on my way. Although I had briefly skimmed through a couple of guide books available locally, nothing could have prepared me for the fascination and sheer diversity of the country I was about to visit.

The River Jordan at Bethany, the site where Christ was baptised, now covered by vegetation. The name Jordan was brought back to Europe by returning crusaders, and reflected in one of our oldest thoroughfares, Jordangate.

The initial four days in Amman produced views of some of the finest Roman sites the world can offer us today. We began with the Citadel on a hill in the centre of Amman, with its impressive theatre below. Next came Um Qais which contains the only black basalt theatre in the world. From the highest point of this ancient city can be seen Lake Tiberius (Sea of Galilee) and a superb view of the Golan Heights.

Here is a meeting of three countries, Israel, Syria and Jordan, reminding me of our Three Shires Head (Derbyshire, Staffordshire & Cheshire). Nor did the reminders cease there, when, after an excellent lunch (Jordanian food is so delicious) we entered the incredible ruins of Jerash. The excavations cover an area almost equal to that of Ephesus in Turkey, but here reconstruction of dozens of columns gives a far greater impression of the atmosphere created by their use. There is a magnificent colonnaded plaza and streets, theatres, temples and later Byzantine churches built on temple sites.

Columns, which inspired our Georgian ancestors in their building projects, such as our superb town hall, but which are so much leaner and taller than their Macclesfield adaptations, create an incredible aura; one in particular has a somewhat awesome credential. Standing adjacent to what is now known as the Cathedral, the column is perpetually in motion, as demonstrated by wedging a coin (10p piece) in the niche between the foot and base on which it stands. Slowly the protruding half of the coin can be seen moving up and down. There is an immediate desire to beat a hasty retreat.

After traversing Mount Nebo, where Moses is said to have been buried, at last my wish was fulfilled with a visit to the River Jordan at Bethany, where Christ was baptised by John the Baptist. Today the river is hardly visible at this point, hidden by vegetation, but Jericho sits in the background adding strength to the view.

After two enjoyable days in Aqaba, Petra, 'the red rose city' was eagerly awaited. A day of exploration followed by a day of digging, made Petra feel truly mine. We uncovered the northeastern portion of the outer wall of the Blue Chapel, a Byzantine chapel so called because of its coloured stones. It sits halfway up from the valley, the centre one of three; the other two chapels are now fully excavated, and the lower one has revealed a very impressive mosaic floor; all circa 1st – 3rd centuries A.D.

The return to Amman brought another wish to fruition when we reached Krak de Montreal, a crusader castle now known as Shaubak, returning my thoughts to Ranulf, Earl of Chester and his Cheshire entourage. It seems that everywhere I travel there is always a reminder of home.

Cockatrice and Sherd Halls

Having mentioned some local connections with the Crusades, last month, it seemed appropriate in this article to look at another possible link. The subject has intrigued and perplexed some members of our local community from time to time – why was there once a hall on the south-eastern side of Mill St. called 'Cockatrice?'

The area of Mill St. where Cockatrice Hall stood circa 1500-1700.

Title deeds for a house, 69 Pickford St., but now demolished, refer to the original plot of land on which it was built as part of a croft called 'Cockapice Croft'. I understand that the deeds relating to the former Quaker Meeting House (now a club) almost hidden behind 86 Mill Street (the present Scope shop) make reference to a Cockatrice Hall on the site. Although I have not seen these deeds yet the name does have a ring of truth to it, which suggests that the clerk, when copying the deeds for the adjoining property, 69 Pickford St. made an error in writing the name (a not infrequent occurrence).

The name of the hall most likely came from a coat of arms which would have been set above the doorway. But what was a cockatrice, and who would have used such a device?

The cockatrice, otherwise known as a basilisk, is a creature of myths and legends. It was considered to be the king of serpents, small and evil with a cock's head, serpent's tail and dragon-like body. Its glittering eyes projected a deathly piercing stare which complimented its ability to poison prey with its venomous breath. The creature, hatched from a cock's egg by a serpent on a dung-hill was, therefore, the most un-likely candidate to be adopted for a coat of arms – and it is a rare device.

Yet adopted it was by a branch of the Langley family, and over the centuries has appeared in various forms e.g. a public house sign in Norfolk, where there was a local connection with a family member. The nearest to Macclesfield include an heraldic tapestry formerly in Bramhall Hall, which sported the arms of Langley of Agecroft impaling Davenport of Bramhall – the result of a marriage between Thomas Langley and Cicely, aunt of Sir William Davenport (circa 1510); also a device in an heraldic window in the south chapel of Cheadle parish church.

In 1533 Robert Langley of Agecroft recorded his arms as a cockatrice, but because of an earlier female inheritance within the family, it has been suggested that the coat of arms was adopted with the inheritance from a family called Pendlebury; however, it is unusual that the family name was not also taken. The interesting point is that Robert Langley had no sons, only four daughters, one of whom, Katharine, married Thomas Legh the fourth son of Sir Piers Legh of Lyme.

A deed of 6th March 1712 refers to lands on the eastern side of Mill Street as 'the inheritance of Earl Rivers, Peter Leigh (Legh) of Lyme Esq. and Edward Swettenham of Sommerford Gent.' and 'certain lands of the Earl of Derby called the placeyard' etc. From previous researches I know that the first block south from the Market Place belonged to Earl Rivers and the next, relating to the old 'castle' site and placeyard (or

A 19th century dinner plate showing clearly a cockatrice as a central design.

Crusade to make him emperor in Constantinople. Nothing materialised, the old emperor was reinstated, but the dynasty was soon ejected from the city by a local faction yet survived in the Trebizond region.

One cannot argue with the thought that the cockatrice was a fitting device for their family coat of arms!

Trebizond was extremely important for the Persian trade, particularly spices, and in the 19th century, when Persian patterns proved popular, the cockatrice was once more 'imported'. Several pottery and porcelain companies used it to decorate tablewares, such as Minton of Stoke-on-Trent.

The cockatrice is not found in France as an emblem, but somehow it found its way early to England and the Langley family; whether by trade or crusade is intriguing. There is a river in Israel between Haifa and Caesarea which was called Cockatrice in the mid-12th century. Our mystery is still with us, but there appears to be plenty of scope for further research.

* * *

Palace yard), the Earl of Derby; and the final area before Park Green, Edward Swettenham; therefore the area belonging to the Leghs of Lyme must have extended somewhere around what is today the Pickford Street area. This would have been an ideal burgage plot on which to build a Tudor hall, entitling the owner to be a freeman of Macclesfield.

Which family originally owned the hall may never be known, but in all probability it was part of a marriage settlement at some point in time, and the Langley connections are certainly there.

The most famous coat of arms bearing a cockatrice is that of the Comnenus family of Trebizond, a port on the Black Sea, now part of Turkey. Alexius I seized power in 1081 (in England the Domesday survey was underway). By 1183 Andronicus Comnenus ruled jointly with the young son of a cousin, whom he forced to sign his mother's death warrant. The young boy was then murdered and Andronicus married the child widow, Agnes of France. His harsh and often cruel reforms did benefit the region, but an aristocrats' revolt brought about his death at the hands of a mob. Another family member became emperor but was blinded by his brother and thrown into prison with his son. The boy escaped to Italy in 1201 and persuaded the Fourth

A Minton cup and saucer 'Pink Cockatrice' design, courtesy of the Minton Museum, proving the pattern is still popular.

Initially I was unable to help with an enquiry regarding the site of Shert or Sherd Hall near Macclesfield, but fortunately managed to obtain some information which indicated that the hall in question had been rebuilt by the early 18th century. It then became Fulshaw Hall and was near Wilmslow not Macclesfield. There is, of course, Sherd Fold Farm on the main road between Tytherington and Adlington, sadly the recent focus in the area of the Foot & Mouth epidemic. No doubt, at some point in time the Sherd family was connected with that particular area, but at present no further details are known.

The enquiry regarding the hall arose from a leaflet produced by the Roman Catholic Diocese of Shrewsbury last year (2000) to mark its 150th anniversary. The information suggested a 'Pilgrims' Trail' and included 'Shert Hall, the family home of Blessed John Shert, on the outskirts of Macclesfield'.

It subsequently transpired that John Shert was educated at Brasenose College, Oxford, to which many local pupils were admitted over the centuries. The college had been founded in 1509 by Dr. Smith, Bishop of Lincoln, and Sir Richard Sutton of the parish of Sutton near Macclesfield. Priority was first given to students from both Prestbury parish (in which Sir Richard resided) and Prescott in Lancashire, (where Dr. Smith was born) before being offered to those in other areas.

Shert was granted his B.A, on 17th January 1567, in the reign of the Protestant queen, Elizabeth I. During the following year a college was founded in Douai, northern France; it was an important centre where a Bible in English was produced for the use of Roman Catholics. Having attended the college, Shert was ordained in Rome and returned to England in August 1578.

This was the time when Mary Queen of Scots was held captive in England under the custody of Bess of Hardwick and her fourth husband, the Earl of Shrewsbury. They were loyal to Elizabeth and the Church of England – hence their unenviable task of keeping the Scottish queen safe and 'occupied'. But Mary's considerable pension from the French government, as widow of the Dauphin, was constantly and surreptitiously used to finance plots against Elizabeth.

The Earl, as Lord Lieutenant, was responsible for law and order; but some of the many plots afoot to set Mary free unfortunately involved a handful of Derbyshire Roman Catholic families, friends of Shrewsbury and related through marriage to Bess. These were important families, yet the Earl had to put duty first.

The Jesuit priests were returning to England from the Continent in effect as missionaries, and one of them, Father Edward Campion, was welcomed into the household of the Derbyshire branch of the Foljambe family. The Earl had no choice but to seek out these recusants and imprison them.

Unfortunately Shert was captured and imprisoned in the Tower of London, whilst the Privy Council tracked down his known associates, including Campion. All were condemned to death, but for some reason Shert's execution was delayed until 28th May 1582. He therefore takes his place as one of the 'Nine Martyrs of the Shrewsbury Diocese'.

Shert Hall is actually recorded as Sherd Hall; variations in spelling often recur with family names throughout history. It seems possible, therefore, that John Shert was related and descended from a Macclesfield branch of the family, for there is a Thomas del Sherd recorded as owning a tenement on Chestergate in February 1406. This branch of the family remained in the town, and Sherds appear as tenants in the Park Green and Park Lane areas of Macclesfield in the 18th century.

In 1722 one of the Pickford family (now remembered by Pickford Street), John, leased the house in Pickford Eyes near Park Green to another, but obviously much later, Thomas Sherd. There was also a workhouse or building built on part of the premises.

Presumably it is the same Thomas Sherd who also appears on both the extant 1743 and 1755-56 Land Tax returns, the latter showing him in possession of a house, value £11 and 11 Cheshire acres (i.e. just over 23 statute acres) of land, value £25. These entries relate to what is now the site of Harvest Printers adjacent to the Park Lane roundabout and were leased from the Cholmondeley family, which was in possession of the vast parkland area at that time.

At the rear of the property was a hemp yard; this was a piece of ground on which hemp was grown. It was invaluable to satisfy the demand for cords, ropes and stout fabrics, the latter necessary for packing and transporting goods. This was the site of the medieval park-keeper's house once in the tenancy of John de Macclesfield.

Meanwhile Thomas Sherd had also leased a barn, stable and garden in Pickford Eyes on

View from the site of the original medieval park-keeper's house looking north. In the 18th century the Sherd family house stood on the site, overlooking the Dams down in the hollow. At that time there were hardly any buildings to be seen, only fields, hedgerows, the Dams Brook flowing down from the north, and a stream winding its way down from South Park crossed by a footbridge on the left, near to the present Halfords car park. In 1775 Charles Roe's church began to take shape on the horizon; but with the great sale of the parkland, from 1788 the view rapidly changed. A population explosion during the following three decades saw buildings mushrooming, and the idyllic pastural view of centuries was swept away.

10th April 1769, which later became the site of the Ryle Bank on the corner of Sunderland Street and Park Green (until recently partly occupied by the Magistrates Court).

By 1775 the surname is shown as Sheard, but should be Sherd, when the Park Lane tenement was taken over from Thomas by his brother Richard (possibly sons of the Thomas who leased earlier in the century). Richard evidently purchased the property, for he is recorded as the owner in 1792, but the hempyard and most of the land had been relinquished earlier.

His will dated 25th March 1811 leaves his estate to his widow Agnes, but allows the two children of his brother, Thomas, from his first marriage, and the present wife and two children of the second, the remaining money. Thomas was to receive 'a clock in the parlour, a watch and clothing, and the 'burial place in the Church Yard' of the Parochial Chapel (now St. Michael's). This branch of the family had evidently forsaken their Roman Catholic beliefs.

* * *

One thing which never fails to surprise is the way in which the study of history can create the most unusual coincidences. A son of my close neighbours has lived in Northern France for several years, and only after writing the above did I discover that he and his family now live in Douai. Thanks to my neighbours' offer of information, a French dictionary and a guide to the town, I was able to appreciate that the college attended by John Shert, known as the College des Grands Anglais and founded 29th September 1568, had, in fact, ceased in 1613. The building subsequently fell into ruin. However, a new college was built in 1745, only to fall prey to the

197

French revolutionaries when it was sequestrated for use as a military hospital in 1793.

The family had been surprised to learn that a possible candidate for their family tree, a Vivian Haydock, together with his son, Richard, had joined the college at Douai in 1573. Vivian was appointed procurator for the college in England in 1581. On his return he met Campion, but, unfortunately, was to be 'hunted from place to place' and, having bad health, soon died.

He was descended from Sir George Haydock, lord of the manors of Haydock (near Warrington), Cottam (near Preston) and several more. His daughter, Joan, married Peter Legh of Lyme in the reign of Henry V (1413-22).

This Peter was the son of Peter Legh beheaded in 1399 for his support of Richard II. The son fought at Agincourt, was knighted on the field, but died in Paris during 1422, having received a wound whilst fighting in the seige of Meaux. His body was brought home for burial in what is now our parish church of St. Michael's, which suggests that the Legh Chapel was created at that time to receive it. This certainly evokes the question, 'Why in the Macclesfield chapel and not Prestbury church?',

after all St. Peter's, Prestbury was the Mother church, yet still under grant to St. Werburgh's Abbey, Chester.

Perhaps it was a political gesture, intended to convey the importance of the chapel and the borough of Macclesfield; Peter Legh was a freeman, and the chapel played an integral part in the municipal life of the borough. (Subsequent information suggests that Peter (Piers) could be buried in a burial mound known as Knight's Low within the Lyme Park estate, and the chapel purely memorial).

His marriage to Joan Haydock meant that for a short period she and Katherine de Kyngeslegh (mistress of John de Macclesfield) were sisters-in-law; Katherine, of course, married Peter's brother, John Legh of Ridge in 1422. Joan subsequently married Sir Richard Molyneaux, ancestor of the Earls of Sefton.

It is also evident that as John Shert attended the English College in Douai during 1576, he would have met both Vivian and Richard Haydock. This conveniently returns me to the Sherds of Macclesfield who eventually owned several properties in the town, the main residence being on the site of the present day

St. George's Street. On the left is the Baptist Church which is in Macclesfield, but the next block of houses on the left (and beyond) are in Sutton parish. The boundary cuts across several streets to reach the top of Hobson Street.

The Bull's Head, Market Place, a property which was on the list of rentals for the Cholmondeley family, together with other properties dotted around the town and several tenanted plots spread out over the vast parkland area.

Harvest Printers, as previously mentioned.

The daughter of yet another neighbour, with a property on St. George's St. adjacent to the former Sherd site, kindly lent me her property deeds in order to help identify the development which had taken place in the area after the great sale of 1788.

The parkland was originally held by the Crown together with Macclesfield manor, and leased to various individuals during the 13th to 15th centuries. However, as previously mentioned, the Savage family (originally from Derbyshire but established in Runcorn by the 16th century), had become investors in the borough and manor from the early 15th century. At some time during the latter half of the 15th century it is apparent that the parkland came into the ownership of the Savages; most likely from some important service rendered to the Crown.

In the early 18th century the land passed to the Cholmondeleys through a marriage settlement, and was eventually used as collateral in acquiring loans to pay off the vast debts relating to the Cholmondeley estate near Nantwich.

This land, together with certain properties in the town, including the Bull's Head in the Market Place, was divided into lots and sold at auction. There were many tenants, some of whom (e.g. the Roe family) managed to buy what they had been renting.

Another family which had risen to prominence during the 18th century was that of Ryle, and about this time John Ryle extended his holdings in the southern part of the town. The St. George's Street deeds confirm that the property, in the parish of Sutton, was included in the Ryle estate, the remainder of which is now South Park.

In 1824 the street name was Great George St., by 1839 it had its present name.

The area was originally part of the Big Mill Field in Sutton and the plot of land on which the house now stands, was sold by John Ryle on 16th August 1823. By June 1824 the St. George's Street house was built and sub-let as an investment property, which it remained until recently. From 1924 to 1932 is was owned by a Mrs. Hannah Johnson who had a business of baker and confectioner at 24 Sunderland Street – a small shop next to the Wesleyan Chapel (now a snooker hall).

The Ryle Family

Henry VIII succeeded to the throne in 1509 at little more than 18 years of age, and at first relied on his father's 'mature councillors'. In April 1512 England was again at war with France and, during the following year, Henry, at the head of a huge army, took charge of the campaign on the soil of northern France. On 16th August 1513 he won the battle of the Spurs near today's Belgium border, but whilst he was thus engaged the King of Scotland, James IV, had declared war and crossed the border into England.

The move had been expected, and Thomas Howard, Earl of Surrey and military commander of the northern provinces, was prepared. He had learnt of the planned attack whilst in Yorkshire and immediately sent out orders to the English nobles of the adjacent counties to meet him with their armed retinues.

Soon an army of 30,000 men gathered, of which 5,000 would eventually die in battle; the Scottish losses would be reported as double those of the English. Unfortunately many from the Macclesfield area, under the banner of Christopher Savage, did not return. And, although the battle lasted only three hours and the English were victorious (James IV was slain in the first assault), Savage himself, who was mayor of Macclesfield at that time, perished in the fray. It was reported that few freemen returned to the town, which would have left wives and children to carry on the day-to-day business in order to survive.

With the small borough in decline for a generation (there is no record of a mayor between 1512 and 1525) it is apparent that young men from other areas, particularly those with whom the former freemen traded, would be encouraged to come and settle here. This could have been either by marriage or by bringing their families with them. A generation later a John Ryle is listed as mayor of Macclesfield (1541-42), and this appears to be the first intimation of the Ryle family having settled in the town. In

Properties adjoining the Memorial Park on Park Green. The area was part of Pickford Eyes or Lower Eyes (i.e. heyes from the medieval period which were enclosures of land). On this site Thomas Royle (his son John used the spelling Ryle for his surname) began his dyeing business in the mid-18th century.

ROYLE HALL.
Burnley

Royle Hall near Burnley in Lancashire, built in the mid-17th century to replace the old hall. The original on the site was said to be the ancestral home of the Royle (or Ryle) family. Until recently the area, adjoining the banks of the River Calder, had long been associated with dyeing.

order to be elected to such an important position, Ryle had obviously arrived some time earlier; but it is interesting to note that whilst the Rowe family (no connection with Charles Roe) continued to play a prominent role in local affairs, the old traditional families of Fallibrome, Liversage and Downes were replaced by the Stapletons and Healeys, amongst others – families from the Lancashire and Yorkshire areas.

This has to be an indication of a local woollen and flax industry which would be supported by local dyers. Because of the abundant water supply, Macclesfield long held the position of an important dyeing centre, and there is little doubt that this was the reason for the advent of John Ryle (or Royle).

Earlier, in the 15th century, the Ryle or Royle family had settled in Styal and Wilmslow, but where had they come from? One suggestion is that the surname derived from the hamlet of Ruyhul in Etchells close by Stockport. Another alternative is that they originated about a mile or so from Burnley in Lancashire, near to Padiham stepping-stones which cross the river Calder. There they had built Royle Hall, a house acquired by the Townley family in the reign of Henry VIII, but rebuilt in the mid-17th century.

Today Royle Road leads towards the site; the original hall was well fortified, situated on a piece of land almost surrounded by water from the Calder and one of its streams. The interesting point is that the area has also long held a reputation for dyeing, and within recent years had an important dyeworks near the site.

For centuries, therefore, the Ryle (or Royle) family had lived in significant dyeing areas where there were good supplies of water, and, although the evidence is at present circumstantial, it does suggest that they were more than likely involved in the industry.

Thomas Royle, who married Martha, daughter of Urian Whilton of Sutton (described as both yeoman and cooper) on 27th May 1744, was certainly a dyer, because he appears as such on property deeds relating to part of the Parsonage Green (now Park Green) area.

By the 18th century the Pickford family owned or leased about a third of the occupied area of Macclesfield and a small part of the adjoining lands in Sutton. A house and barn stood on part of the Lower Eyes or Pickford Eyes; the site today is the strip of land between Brook Street and the Memorial Park on Park Green. The house most likely stood adjacent to today's Sunderland Street with the barn at the rear, nearer the River Bollin. Both were leased by Pickford to a Robert Nickson, but in March 1743 Martha's father took over the lease. After Urian's death the lease was transferred to Thomas and Martha 'Royle' on 13th June 1752, comprising a close 66ft. wide (about 20 metres) and 101ft. long (31 metres) and buildings.

By May 1768 Thomas had built a dyehouse on the site and renewed the lease for 999 years. This was the start of a very lucrative business which, by the end of the 18th century, would create for the family an important position in Macclesfield affairs.

Civil Duties

After the traumas of the 17th century civil wars, suddenly a reawakening took place in England; the country took a considerable step forward in developing and 'modernising', and nowhere more so than in Macclesfield.

The Royalist Ryle family had survived (a list of 'delinquents' i.e. known activists against Parliament in 1648 included a Reynold Ryle from Macclesfield Hundred) and, as mentioned, by the middle of the 18th century Thomas Royle (Ryle) had established a dyeworks on the south-east corner of Park Green.

Royle died aged 59 years on 20th December 1779 and was buried at Christ Church with his surname recorded as 'Ryle'. It is interesting to note that his wife's father, Urian, was probably a Quaker, which could explain why their eldest son, John, (born 1745) was inclined more towards a simplified Church of England service rather than High Church rituals.

John was mayor for the year 1773-74, and members of the corporation (the Mayor, Aldermen & Burgesses) attended the Parochial Chapel of St. Michael's (now the Parish Church). However, when Charles Roe's church had been completed and consecrated, this branch of the Ryle family became communicants at the 'New Church', as it was originally known.

During John Ryle's mayoralty, on Easter Day 3rd April 1774, the preacher John Wesley arrived in the town 'just in time . . . to walk to the old church with the mayor'. For some considerable time afterwards, the Ryles welcomed Wesley into their home on his return visits.

Wesley had first appeared in the town in November 1745, just before the fateful intrusion of Bonnie Prince Charlie and his troops. But whereas the latter was considered an unwelcomed intruder, the former was viewed by many almost as a saint. He rarely missed a visit to the area each year from the 1760s until his death in 1791, and during his April visit of 1776 Charles Roe's niece, Hester, spent time with him 'at old Mr. Ryle's'.

Unfortunately Wesley's words could be harsh at times, almost cruel, and there were those fanatics who, in presenting his cause, drummed up fears of a puritanical revival; memories were long and no one wanted another great schism within the Church, not even Wesley.

After Thomas's death, his son, John Ryle Snr. did continue his close association with Wesley,

and the latter's journal records that on Monday 16th July 1787 he viewed 'Mr. Ryle's silk-mill' which he noted 'keeps 250 children in perpetual employment'. This refers to the impressive building on Park Green recently vacated by Gradus Ltd. and built in 1785 as recorded on one of the rain-water heads.

This is significant, because the assumption has always been that Daintry and Ryle built the mill. The book *East Cheshire Textile Mills* notes 'The evidence for the primary process of Park Green Mill, Macclesfield is not clear' but suggests that at that time it was a cotton mill.

When the grandson of John Ryle Snr. prepared his autobiographical notes, he wrote 'My grandfather, John Ryle (Snr) made an immense fortune in the silk trade'. When referring to his father, John Ryle Jnr. he writes that one of his father's sisters married John Smith Daintry and 'her husband was my father's partner in the bank'. However, Daintry eventually borrowed £100,000 from John Ryle Jnr. to create a large 'cotton works' in Manchester – the business failed and forced John Ryle Jnr. into bankruptcy with the failure of the bank in 1841.

The original Mill Lane section of the silk mill was built much earlier than the main section on Park Green. This Mill Lane portion was destroyed by fire in the 1970s but has been rebuilt. The most likely synopsis is that when Thomas Ryle died he left a substantial dyehouse to his son, John Ryle Snr. on Mill Lane, in addition to the original one. Ryle Snr. then added the large section on Parsonage Green (today Park Green), in 1785 as a silk mill. This conclusion is supported by deeds relating to Sutton Mills on Cross St. (now converted into flats).

Michael Daintry and John Ryle Jnr., having taken over the Hawkins and Mills bank (i.e. the Roe banking company) by October 1799, were by 1803 in a position to buy the Sutton water corn mills, and a considerable amount of property and surrounding land in the Mill Green area, from the Earl and Countess of Lucan. However, the deed states that they were not to disturb John Ryle's soughs and his water supply (received as waste water from the Sutton mills) to his 'Silk Mills and Dyehouses' further down the watercourse.

This proves conclusively that John Jnr. had inherited his father's large silk mill and dyeworks and was the sole owner.

The East Cheshire mills survey also refers to a 'double-cylinder atmospheric engine' supplied

The Park Green mill built in 1785 by John Ryle Snr. His son, John Jnr. formed a partnership with Michael Daintry in a banking business, by which they invested in other concerns. However, the story that Daintry and Ryle built the Park Green mill is incorrect.

by Francis Thompson of Chesterfield to Michael Daintry, for a cotton mill in Macclesfield during 1793.

The home of the Daintry family was Leek. Reverend John Daintry had moved from the village of Endon to Leek, where he remained vicar until his death in 1758. His son, John, is recorded as a merchant of Leek in 1773/74 and already had connections with prominent silk manufacturers in Macclesfield. 'Mr. and Mrs. Daintry of Leek' are recorded as great friends of the Roe family, but this probably relates to Michael Daintry Snr. whose son (or nephew?) married into the Ryle family.

By 1810 the younger Daintry and John Ryle Jnr., probably in their capacity as bankers, had entered into partnership with their Wood brothers-in-law and others. Shortly afterwards, on part of the Sutton corn mills site, the partnership built a cotton mill, and with further development converted the corn mills into cotton mills, parts of which were tenanted. As this cotton business did not precede 1803, the mys-

tery of where the 1793 atmospheric engine was installed, at present remains a mystery.

John Ryle Jnr.

John Ryle Jnr. was almost a Christmas baby, for he was born on 9th December 1783. At the time of his birth he had four surviving sisters (originally there were six, but two had died as babies) though only one brother, Thomas, then five years of age.

Grandfather, Thomas, had created an important dye business, but had died four years earlier. John's father, also called John, had been able to build on Thomas's success by adding an impressive silk mill to the complex in 1785, when young John was little more than a year old.

Brother, Thomas, as heir to the Ryle fortune and business, would be destined for great things, and educated accordingly. However, in January 1791 he died at the age of only 12 years, which would have been a considerable blow to the family. (His nephew, John Charles, gives his uncle Thomas's age as 21 years at the

Later Victorian view ('Co-op' celebration) of the area known from the medieval period as the Eyes. In the 17th and 18th centuries it was owned by the Pickford family, one of whom married a Miss Sunderland – hence the name Sunderland Street, a thoroughfare laid out in the late 18th century. Soon the Ryle family leased most of the land in the foreground with permission to build on certain plots. However, all was lost with bankruptcy in 1841. By 1860 the Co-operative Society had started a 'take-over' and remain the owners to this day. Photo reproduced by kind permission of Cheshire Record Office.

time of death, but the Christ Church register records Thomas's birth as 10th June 1778, died 10th January 1791)

This was an age when children had to grow up quickly and many, as young as 16 years, would find themselves in charge of considerable enterprises, so Thomas's training towards entering the family business would have been well advanced. With Thomas's death the responsibility of continuing the family business now fell upon John Jnr.'s shoulders, and the young man was fortunate in marrying Susannah Hurt of Wirksworth, granddaughter of Sir Richard Arkwright, inventor of the spinning-jenny. In all they had three sons and ten daughters, but only two sons and five daughters would survive to grow up and marry.

Sunderland Street

In the same year as the silk mill was built i.e. on 23rd. Aug 1785 John Ryle Snr. agreed with Joseph Pickford of Royton, Lancashire for a lease of a large area of land, part of Lower Eyes, recorded as 4,193 yards. It was bounded on the west by Sunderland Street; on the east by 'the brook' (the river Bollin); on the north by Townley Street and on the south by the land already leased by John Snr. as an inheritance from his father, Thomas. Today it is the site of the former Beehive Restaurant, including the remainder of the block, on the corner of Brook Street and Sunderland Street; there Ryle intended to build a house.

There were certain commitments which were part of the lease; John Snr. had to contribute towards the repairs of the streets in the area; allow rights of way to and from the various silk mills; keep the sewers 'scowered and cleased', whilst 'keeping in repair' the cart bridge erected at the northern end of Sunderland Street (where the Dams Brook joined the Bollin).

About this time also, it appears that John Snr. leased a further plot of land on the opposite side of Sunderland Street, the front of which faced Parsonage Green (Park Green). At the rear there was a garden with a barn and the property had previously been the residence of Thomas Sherd, (mentioned above). At this time it was purely an investment and tenanted.

Ryle's Park Estate

John Snr. must have now begun to feel financially secure, for on 7th March 1788 he purchased from Lord Cholmondeley a considerable area of land, which had been under lease to a 'Mr. Langford'. This appears to be Harry Lankford, a former partner of a group which had continued the business of silk throwsting in Charles Roe's original mill on Parsonage Green. Unfortunately Lankford had been declared bankrupt in 1774 and was, therefore, presumably unable to purchase his former holdings at the time of the 'Great Sale' of the parkland in 1788.

This large area of land, the residue of which is now South Park, became the Ryle estate with Park House built on the site of the present pavilion and cafe. Here John Jnr. brought his bride, and this is where John Charles was born on 10th May 1816. The land at that time stretched down to Parsonage Green, and a lodge and entrance gates were built on the site of the present Harvest Printers, which allowed access to carriages along an original right of way across part of the parkland. The pool, which became known as Ryle's pool, was created to complete the vista from the house.

John Ryle Snr. had died on 16th June 1808 a very wealthy man, and John Jnr. inherited. Later John Charles would write 'My grandfather was the only Ryle who ever attained great wealth, and my father was the first Ryle who left Cheshire, after losing every penny of it'.

Holidays

John Charles was the fourth of six children who enjoyed a happy childhood. Holidays were mostly spent at Bridlington where their father had a yacht called Seaflower. Every morning the children were taken for a walk along the pier, and each given a large biscuit; John Charles recalled one occasion when a great black Newfoundland dog, as tall as himself, snatched the biscuit from his hand. They picnicked on Flamborough Head whilst enjoying the smell from the surrounding turnip fields.

Just once they visited Crosby near Liverpool and travelled back from Runcorn to Manchester on the Bridgewater Canal boat; the journey took a whole day.

But most of all they enjoyed Christmas Eve in Park House, where a yule log, a yule cheese, posset (a drink of hot milk flavoured with sugar or spices to which was added ale, wine or liquor) and an enormous apple pie 'appeared'. They danced country dances in the kitchen with the servants 'to the music of a dulcimer'. The male servants joined the labourers, gardeners and farm workers in the tenants' hall to sing songs, the two favourites being 'John Barleycorn' and 'the Cheshire Cheese'.

The children stayed up until after the clock had chimed twelve and the waits (singers of carols at Christmas and songs at New Year for money) had sung at the hall door. John Charles, in old age, nostalgically recalled them singing 'Christians Awake' some 52 years before.

Sutton Boundary

When considering the parish of Sutton many think of the village or small township concentrated around Sutton Lane Ends, with 'The Lamb Inn' as its 'local'. Newcomers to Macclesfield might be surprised to discover just how far the Sutton parish boundary extends in parts, particularly near Park Green.

Whereas many boundaries have a clearly defined line, the northern part of the Sutton boundary, contiguous with Macclesfield town, meanders across several streets which join Park Street and the lower section of Park Lane, in a somewhat haphazard manner. What was clearly defined before 1788 has, with modern development, become a modern day puzzle. Yet reference to the old parkland area, owned by the Cholmondeleys, soon reveals the old units of division into fields and crofts etc.

These were leased to many individuals and were known by several different, but often very interesting, names e.g. the Lower Dams, the Higher Dams and so forth. Even to this day local residents still refer to the area centred on the Churchill Way roundabout, in the 'dip' near B & Q and Topps Tiles, as 'The Dams'.

But the great sale of 1788 completely altered the landscape in the southern part of the town and, of course, over the boundary into Sutton, due mostly to the endeavours of John Ryle Snr. As already mentioned he bought several units to create his estate, but surprisingly he died intestate on 16th June 1808 leaving his elder son, John, to claim his inheritance as heir-at-law.

Part of the land in Sutton was acquired with help from the Daintry family, probably because of the development of Sutton Mills from corn to textile manufacture. It was always important to keep in mind the future; water rights and rights of way were vital, so it was often easier and cheaper to buy adjoining land when the opportunity arose, than have to pay dearly for access or be taken to court for trespass etc. at a later date.

John Ryle Snr. purchased an area known as 'The Big Mill Field' which covered more than 5 acres. It lay between the plot known as the 'Hempeyard' (extending behind Harvest Printers) and Mill Lane, and seems to have extended to Mill Green. This was not part of his parkland estate, although it ran along the eastern border, but seems to have been bought purely as an investment.

The Wesleyan Influence

John Ryle Snr. had always welcomed Rev. John Wesley on his visits to the town and his manufacturing neighbours on Sunderland Street, the Pearsons, were also Wesleyan devotees; in fact George Pearson (1718-1807) is credited with being 'the real founder of Methodism in Macclesfield'.

In 1769 Pearson, with his partner, George Hordern, had built a silk mill now occupied by Arighi Bianchi & Co. as a warehouse on Sunderland Street next to the railway station. However, in 1787 John Ryle Snr. bought the business for £1,500 as part of his expansion in the area. But earlier in 1779 he had allowed the small Wesleyan chapel to be built almost between the two holdings; this was enlarged in 1799.

Ryle, with others, had been a trustee for the 'Old Chapel' which had stood on part of Arighi Bianchi's Commercial Road site for several years, but with an increase in membership it had become inadequate. Ryle had not provided the land for the old chapel, as previously assumed, but was now able to provide for a more substantial new building.

With his death, son John, although a supporter of Christ Church, was able to assist the Methodist cause further when, on 30th June 1824, he sold 3,170 'superficial square yards' of The Big Mill Field to Rowland Gould for £800. Gould, an alderman, had been mayor of Macclesfield during 1777-78 and again in 1817-18. Immediately the site was cleared and a chapel built in less than three months. It was named Brunswick – as were other Methodist chapels in other areas, and streets – probably in memory of Frederick

William, Duke of Brunswick (N. Germany), brother of George IV's wife, Caroline. Despite the fact George treated his wife with utter contempt, even denying her place in his Coronation of 1820, yet her supporters were numerous.

Frederick brought troops to England and fought alongside Wellington in the Peninsular War in Spain, but was killed during the battle of Ligny, Belgium, where Napoleon defeated Blucher's forces, two days before Waterloo.

With German Protestantism very much akin to Methodism one can well understand the support shown for the House of Brunswick and such a hero, whilst at the same time demonstrating to the King their disapproval of his actions with regard to his wife. Whilst a new street on the eastern side of the chapel was named Lord Street; on the south Bridge Street (now Chapel Street) the one on the west became Great (not King) George Street. There is, perhaps, a hint of lampooning here when considering George IV's enormous torso by this time! The name became a respectable St. Georges within a few years.

On 24th September 1824 Gould sold the land and chapel to Thomas Allen, Gent., and other trustees, for the Wesleyan Methodists. Amongst

The entrance to the former Brunswick Chapel on Chapel St. built 1824.

Former Wesleyan Chapel, Sunderland St., built 1779, enlarged 1799.

them were three silk manufacturers, dyers, an ironmonger, a grocer and a linen draper etc. Six months later (18th March 1825) they borrowed £3,300 (almost half a million pounds today) from John Ryle Jnr., but part came from George Pearson Jnr.'s estate.

In 1850 new trustees were appointed and on 28th May 1889 the chapel estate was accepted in trust by the Charity Commission. A revised list of trustees was then drawn up, and again in 1924 and 1948. But with changing times the final meeting took place in 1971, and the property was sold in 1988 for conversion into apartments.

* * *

My thanks go to Derek Hill, antique dealer, for offering sight of the deeds. Derek can boast a four times mayor of Macclesfield on his family tree; Frederick Hill, born 20th December 1851

died 10th May 1902. He lived at Ellesmere, Buxton Road, and was a pawnbroker and jeweller on Oxford Street Manchester, but also had premises in the Market Place, Macclesfield.

The Bank

For many years, from the 1760s, the Roe & Co. brass and copper business, acted as a bank. During 1787 one of the partners, Edward Hawkins Snr., decided to create an independent bank; he took into the partnership another company partner, Abraham Mills, and shortly afterwards his own nephew.

With the consent of the remaining copper company partners, the bank was moved from the business premises on Macclesfield Common to a more convenient location in the centre of town (i.e. Jordangate, the section which is now part of the Market Place), but by 1797, Napoleon

Bonaparte's activities on the Continent were beginning to create economic difficulties in Britain.

As we have already seen, John Ryle Snr. was weathering the 'storms' well, for, ironically, the wars with France meant a dearth of French silks, which many people had previously preferred, and gave a boost to the British industry. There was also the advantage of lucrative contracts with the Admiralty for large kerchiefs worn by sailors (these were subsequently superseded by the traditional sailor collar).

Ryle and apparently Michael Daintry (although it could have been his son John Smith) were tempted to take over the bank and Roe & Co. guaranteed financial support, but by October 1799 the latter had to withdraw because they too were beginning to feel the effects of economic depression.

As previously mentioned, some years earlier, John Ryle Snr., after extending his interests in the Sunderland Street area, once more encroached on Parsonage (Park) Green. Actually it was his brother-in-law, Samuel Wood, acting as trustee who acquired the lease in 1790 for the corner property, (later 32 Park Green).

Daintry and Ryle never operated from the Jordangate premises, but whether or not they began the banking business at the Parsonage

Green corner is difficult to say, the only definite fact on the deeds is that just after the Napoleonic Wars, the Savings Bank was on the corner site in 1816. By then the two partners appearing on the property deeds were John Smith Daintry and John Ryle Jnr.

Both had inherited vast fortunes and estates from their fathers; John Ryle Snr, had died in 1808 followed by Michael Daintry in 1815. (Michael Daintry had lived to a great age, at least until his early 80s. but his son, Michael, had died young, therefore his only surviving son was John Smith Daintry who had married one of John Ryle's daughters)

Also it was another brother-in-law, Charles Wood, who persuaded John Ryle Jnr. to advance £100,000 for the building of a large cotton works in Manchester. John Smith Daintry and John Ryle Jnr. had opened a large bank in Manchester (from which the investment in the cotton enterprise was made) and presumably operated the Macclesfield bank as a branch of the larger business.

Michael Daintry died a multi-millionaire by today's standards. He left three estates, one in Macclesfield where for a time his son had lived, one in Leek, and his main residence 'Byrons'. By 1816 his son John Smith Daintry, married and with a family, was living at Foden Bank.

The corner site occupied by Ryle's Savings Bank in 1816.

Now site of The Royal Bank of Scotland, this was part of a bakery complex in the late 18th century.

The Bakery

At this time diagonally opposite the bank on Parsonage Green (by coincidence partly occupied today by the Royal Bank of Scotland) was a bakery. The site was part of that acquired by John Ryle Snr in 1788 from Lord Cholmondeley. The bakery, comprising a bakehouse, warehouse, stables, summerhouse and garden, was owned by the baker John Clulow. On 1st March 1793 Ryle allowed Clulow an additional piece of land which had been part of an 'Old Road, running behind the premises but 'then lately stopped up & converted by an Order of Justices & part of a certain field belonging to John Ryle'. Clulow had built two stables and outbuildings on the land and was given permission for his workmen to take carts into the field for collecting coal, hay and straw and 'carry away soil & manure for necessaries, haystalls, etc.'On 1st March 1803 Clulow purchased the land from Ryle Snr.

Upton Hall

The year after his father's death, Ryle Jnr. was mayor (1809-10). On 27th March 1817 he bought Upton Hall, a farm, for £21,000. There his young son, John Charles, loved to ride the asses and donkey. One time he took the four year old boy to help plant a lime tree at the top of the hill, but whilst travelling home late in the evening young John Charles fell off his mount in the gloom, and it was some time before his father realised he was leading a riderless donkey.

In 1837 the family left Park House when John Ryle Jnr. bought the Henbury Estate of almost 1,000 acres for £54,000. John Charles was sent to Oxford to study law, but left to take up employment in his father's Macclesfield bank, and at the same time became a county magistrate.

In June 1841 disaster struck; the London banking agent stopped payment, forcing the Ryles to do likewise 'and every single acre and penny' belonging to the Ryles was used to satisfy creditors. John Charles went to friends in the New Forest, found his vocation and became a Church of England minister; he eventually received a great tribute, after years of hard work and authorship, by becoming the first Bishop of Liverpool.

Shakespeare House

At the time of the Macclesfield Common Enclosure (finalised 1804), the road leading out of town towards Buxton from Waters Green resembled a medium sized track until it reached what is now Fence Avenue and Flint Street. A much-favoured route was up Lunt Hill (now Windmill Street) turning left along Black Road, and finally joining Buxton Road to continue the uphill struggle towards Teg's Nose.

Above: Shakespeare House, Buxton Road.

Right: The initials of William and Maria Cullen who built the inn in 1825.

Today's Buxton Old Road was then the only main route leading to the ancient spa. One allotment of 3 roods and 18 perches (they varied considerably in size) and numbered 220, was in a desirable position, because along its south-west boundary ran the Buxton Road. The plot was reserved in the Enclosure plan for Thomas Bailey who decided to purchase; after his death it passed to his heirs, one of whom was a Richard Leversidge.

In 1822 an Act was passed incorporating a provision for making a new road from the Waters to Buxton. It followed Buxton Road as we know it today, but branched off left immediately below plot 220 to become Buxton New Road (i.e. A537) and was completed during 1824.

By 1825 a William Cullen and wife, Maria, owned the allotment with the intension of investing in a profitable business. The exact date of their occupation is not known but must have been a little earlier, for it was probably their influence which persuaded the owner of the Eddisbury estate, overlooking their land from higher up the hill, to grant them an important concession.

One year earlier (about the time the new road was completed) T.S. Daintry, Esq. owner and resident of Eddisbury Hall, had allowed the overflow from his spring water supply to be diverted through several fields, including a circuitous detour through plot 220, until the water finally reached Knight's Pool further down in the valley.

Ideally situated between the old and new roads, and now in possession of an excellent water supply, the Cullens began to build on and develop the site. To this day the initials and date above the main entrance to the house – 'WMC 1825' – remain as testimony to their achievement.

Although William did not die for a further 6 years, he prepared his will on 27th August 1834, leaving his goods and the house, known 'by the sign of the Shakespeare' (this confirms it was an inn), with the garden and small field to his wife. She also took over the payment due on each 2nd February for 'the trespass on the New Buxton Road'.

Extant directories of the period first list the 'Shakespear Inn' Buxton Road in 1848, but directories can be misleading, and whilst useful as indicators, further research is always necessary. The circumstantial evidence suggests that the Cullens built the house as an inn, and were certainly using it as such in 1834. When William died in 1840, Maria and their son, also named William, soon moved out and let the business to a Charles Mitchell. They must have made a small fortune, for Maria retired to Walworth in Surrey and young William became a druggist (chemist).

Mitchell appears as landlord of the Shakespeare in both the 1848 and 1850 directories. The popularity of the inn seems to have inspired a namesake, for the 1850 list also includes a James Wood, landlord of another 'Shakespear' in Duke Street. It is possibly Mitchell, intent on creating an Elizabethan atmosphere, who was responsible for stones sporting Roman numerals and purporting to be 16th century, now remaining in the cellar, however, prior to 1825 the plot was virgin land.

Maria died in 1849 intestate, but her son received administration of her estate and so became owner of the inn. Just before her death the new owner of the Eddisbury estate, a Mr. Gibbon, tried to stop the water supply by turning it into the Blackbrook course; William Cullen wrote to him and all was well till 1866, when the estate 'passed into the hands of Messrs. Edmonds. London'. The watercourse was then 'racked up', though Cullen was given permission to lay 4 inch glazed pipes through their grounds and conduct the water to his premises.

Two years later the estate was sold off in lots, and the purchaser of the field where the spring rises 'made a determined effort to interfere with its course' but without success. That year suffered a very bad drought yet the spring did not dry up; however, the problems with the water supply could have been the cause of Charles Mitchell leaving the inn. He was no longer there by the early 1870s and a rambler in 1878 wrote:

'To a visitor in Macclesfield, few places are more interesting for the variety of scenery which may be met with, than a walk for a few miles on either the old or new roads to Buxton; but of the two the new way is better adapted for a pedestrian ramble, on account of more easy ascent. It turns to the left of the point of junction of both ways, from what was formerly a much-frequented public-house called the Shakespeare Inn, now a private residence.'

The Cullens had returned; this time William remained there in retirement until his death on 29th September 1877. His widow, Martha, retained the property but in 1890 gave 'Shakespeare Cottage' to her much loved nephew, Peter Walker, 'a servant man' of Buxton Rd. He let the premises, became a farmer at Ridge Hill Foot, Sutton, but in 1918 sold 'Shakespeare House' to a butcher of Hurdsfield Road. The property once more became owner occupied when the butcher died and within a year his daughter married.

Although passing through several hands for almost a century 'Shakespeare House' has retained its name and, of course, its own interesting history.

The 'junction of both ways, from what was formerly a much-frequented public-house called the Shakespeare Inn, now a private residence'.

Somerford Chapel – Shakerley Family

Whilst travelling through Congleton towards Astbury, but then turning right along the A54 to Holmes Chapel, one passes on the right-hand side lands which were once part of the Somerford estate.

Hidden from view, along a narrow and initially meandering track culminating in a farmer's field, is an old but impressive chapel, at one time belonging to the estate. Now under the auspices of the Diocese of Chester (services take place on a periodic basis), it is very much appreciated and cared for by members of the Caravan and Camping Club as part of their activities in the area. It was originally built by one of the Shakerleys and provides yet another facet of local history.

The Shakerley family's ancestral home was in Lancashire during the Tudor Period when one of them married the widow of John Legh of Booths and so moved into the area. Their home became Hulme Hall two miles south-west of Nether Peover. Further generations developed the site, but it was a marshy area of land, conducive to creating a moat though not a healthy lifestyle.

By the early 19th century, although the moat remained and the original kitchen with a few dilapidated outbuildings, the property had been totally rebuilt leaving no clues as to its original appearance. The Shakerleys were no longer resident, and had in fact moved a century earlier.

The story begins in the early 17th century when one of the sons, Peter, married Margaret, daughter of William Oldfield of Bradwell, Derbyshire. These were the years of religious unrest in England but the Oldfields, a significant family entitled to a coat of arms, were staunch Royalist and C. of E.; in fact one of them Rev. John Oldfield was ejected by the Parliamentarians at the start of the Civil War.

Sir Geoffrey, heir of Sir Peter and Margaret, and still of Hulme Hall, fought on the side of the Royalists. Perhaps remembering the treatment of those within his mother's family (and possibly his own, for his sister had married the vicar of Mobberley) he took action against a Dissenting minister who continued preaching in Bosley chapel after the Restoration. The minister, John Garside, had not conformed to the Church of England principles, and as it had been necessary to pass a law in order to re-establish authority within the Church, any minister in breach of the law had to stand trial.

There had been many problems as Dissenting ministers had stood outside the gates of churches trying to persuade people not to join the congregation. Garside had no chance against the powerful personality of Sir Geoffrey; the latter pulled him out of the pulpit, escorted him to Chester and saw him put in prison for a spell.

It is interesting to note that Sir Geoffrey's first wife, Katherine, was the daughter of William Pennington of Muncaster, Cumberland. The Penningtons were involved with mining in the 18th century, but at this early date Sir Geoffrey's connections forged links between the two regions, as friends, relatives and retainers travelled to and fro.

Sir Geoffrey became trustee in an important marriage settlement dated 30th April 1672, between Phillip, son of Edward Swettenham, and Elizabeth, the eldest daughter of Edward Wilson of Dallam Tower, Westmorland. The contract was for a considerable sum of £1,000 to Edward Wilson for his daughter. As security Swettenham Hall, with its adjoining lands, mills, cottages etc. in Somerford Booths, together with properties in Macclesfield Town (i.e. the site of the present library on Jordangate and property on Mill Street) and 'elsewhere' in Cheshire were included.

Sir Geoffrey died on 6th April 1673 and his place was taken by son, Peter, who became an M.P., Governor of Chester, and acquired the Somerford estate from his grandmother's family, the Oldfields. A female descendant wrote in 1947 that he had 'bought' it from 'a family by the name of Oldfield', presumably without realising the 17th century connection by marriage.

Although still in possession of Hulme Hall, Sir Peter began to build a new mansion in Somerford, which was mostly completed by 1720. Together with his wife, Elizabeth, daughter of a close neighbour, Sir Thomas Mainwaring 1st. bart, of Over Peover, he moved into his new residence and attended services in the lovely old church of Astbury, as they now lived within its parish. Unfortunately a dispute occurred, and

Sir Peter, whose family pew was west of the Lady Chapel accessed by an adjoining small side door, quarrelled with the vicar, saw the door bricked up, and retaliated by building the private chapel (1725) in his own grounds.

For the next 200 years the Shakerleys 'cherished' their chapel, enhanced their estate, preserved the park and famous herd of white cattle descended from those on the Derbyshire hills, which resembled Chillingham cattle but without horns.

The house no longer exists; the chapel interior has undergone some alteration, yet still reflects the family connections and penchant in an appealing way. And whilst, through modern eyes, we might view the actions of Sir Geoffrey and Sir Peter as somewhat amusing, yet we do well to remember the remaining memorials of Sir Geoffrey Charles Shakerley D.S.O. Lt. Col. (1869-1915) and his two brothers, all killed in action on French soil during the First World War.

The death knell had also tolled for the estate, but fortunately not the chapel, which, after the death of Sir Walter, 3rd. bart. in 1943, was given as a chapel of ease to Astbury and dedicated to All Saints by the Bishop of Chester on 13th April 1947.

Above: The chapel of All Saints, Somerford.

Below: The west end of the chapel sporting a wooden cupola with a bell. The large clock has a wooden face, the mechanism of which formerly 'struck the hours on the chapel bell.'

Buttons

When I was growing up in Pendle Witches' country there was a shop close by where time had stood still. It was a Victorian shop full of buttons, buckles, fastenings of all kinds and hair combs etc., and almost half the stock looked as though it had been in situ since the premises first opened for business.

Known as 'The Button Shop' it fascinated and delighted, and I always saw it as the next best thing to Aladdin's cave. It must have been all those wonderful visits which inspired me to take an interest in buttons; an interest which has never waned.

One can imagine my surprise and delight when, on arriving in Macclesfield some 35 years ago, I discovered that the town had been famous for producing buttons. During my researches I have, therefore, always kept a lookout for any mention of these useful, often decorative and sometimes highly significant accoutrements, which in today's world of zips and Velcro seem to be vying for preservation amongst so many more interesting and irreplaceable objects from the past.

Buttons, in one form or another, have been around for centuries. Ancient Greeks, and the Etruscan tribe of Italy, all used buttons and loops to fasten tunics at the shoulders. The ancient tribes of Europe preferred brooches, clasps or pins but, with the invention of buttonholes in the 13th century, the craze for fashionable buttons took off. They competed with items of jewellery to display affluence; and as the centuries progressed all sorts of ingenious materials (i.e. ivory, tortoiseshell, mother of pearl etc.) were fashioned into the most elaborate designs, to adorn and facilitate the wearing of clothes.

By the 18th century button-making, like most manufacturing of that period, had become an art. The French, and later Japanese, produced exquisite hand-painted porcellaneous sets, whilst Bohemia (Czechoslovakia) became renowned for brilliantly coloured glass varieties.

Nor did we English lag behind, thanks mainly to entrepreneurs such as Matthew Boulton, who monopolised the London luxury market by using unique materials e.g. Blue John stone from Derbyshire and Wedgwood cameos. However, a far greater market existed for military and everyday utilitarian varieties.

Although buttons must have been in vogue in earlier periods, to date the first evidence of them in the Macclesfield area appears in early 17th wills and Court Records, and two wills in particular are of great importance viz. Stephen Row(e) (1617) and Richard Blacklach (1635). Both were extremely important and wealthy merchants; the latter lived in the remains of John de Macclesfield's residence on Mill Street

Their inventories include stocks of horse or ox hair and linen thread buttons, many black; but whereas Stephen Rowe had on hand only four 'great gross' of Spanish silk buttons, two decades later Blacklach's stock included many more Spanish imports comprising cloaks, cloak buttons and coloured buttons.

Perhaps the growing popularity of Spanish silk buttons inspired a desire to produce alternatives locally. During the Commonwealth Period in

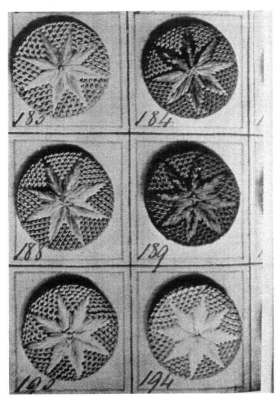

18th century Macclesfield silk buttons as produced by the Brocklehurst family, courtesy of Macclesfield Museums Trust.

Philadelphia – an 18th century port, destination of hundreds of bags of local buttons, including 'Death heads', for distribution into its hinterland, particularly to Fort Pitt (now Pittsburg).

1655 the industry received considerable encouragement from the Burgesses when legislation was brought in to curb 'foreigners and strangers' bringing their buttons into the Borough and selling them at much reduced prices.

By then local manufacture had greatly increased, but was still using mostly linen thread, horse or ox hair. At times the importation of silk was spasmodic, however by the 18th century more was being used and also considerable amounts of mohair, especially by Charles Roe and the Brocklehursts. (Buttons were in great demand – I have counted more than 60 on a dress coat c. 1760 displayed in Powis Castle).

As the century progressed silk buttons fell out of favour, despite legislation, and one significant property deed is full of fascinating and intriguing information. It relates to a property in 'Church Yard Side' adjacent to the Parochial Chapel (now the Parish Church) which belonged to Samuel Stokes, button merchant and chapman. He operated with other family members and a network of factors as far afield as London, Aberdeen, Dublin, Belfast, and locally. Suppliers of raw materials were in Liverpool, Manchester, Bolton, Stockport, Leek and again the Macclesfield environs.

By 1770 Stokes, considerably in debt, was bankrupted; all 100 items of stock on hand were listed and the property subsequently sold. Apart from a variety of haberdashery there were several horn buttons and moulds, usually attributed to Sheffield, and many bags of buttons. Almost the largest item was '275 bags of 2 Cord Death head Buttons', other bags contained 2 or 3 cords of different sizes, and their moulds.

The death's head ones are a mystery. I have followed them via Birmingham and the Port of London to Philadelphia and beyond. Ladings of 1763-64 (on behalf of Baynton, Wharton & Morgan, the chief suppliers of Fort Pitt) whilst showing many bags of silk and twist buttons etc. always list the Death heads separately e.g. 30th August 1763 '133 bags of Scarlet Death head Coat and Breast Buttons'. Why so popular?

No one seems to know, they are even unknown to the V&A. costume department; however a Harrisburg archivist (near Pittsburg) confirms that whilst some military buttons did sport the death's head, they were always metal and 19th century, but suggests the scarlet ones were possibly for Freemasons. Perhaps 18th century portraits would solve the mystery, but which lodges could help?

215

Dieulacres Abbey

Many (many!) years ago I remember taking lunch in a guest-house, high up in the Italian Alps, which had a sign outside proudly proclaiming 'Napoleon neither ate, drank nor slept here'; which, by virtue of the fact I have mentioned Napoleon, allows me the opportunity to mention a recent visit to St. Helena, the last abode of the French Emperor.

The island, situated in a remote part of the South Atlantic, with its nearest neighbour, Ascension Island, lying 700 miles north-east, could not possibly have reminded me of Macclesfield; how wrong I was.

In 1824, the governor, Brigadier-General Walker, a distinguished officer who had previously served in Bombay, India, for the East India Company (which at that time was still in charge of the island before shortly being supplanted by the British Government) decided to introduce silk-worms to boost the island's economy. A supply was ordered from India, but the creatures were dead on arrival.

One of the Chinese labourers, first brought to the island during the Napoleonic Wars in 1810 from Canton, offered to return home and bring some worms with him. Permission was given and a silk farm established at 'The Briars', which today is the home of the French Consul.

The latter stems from the fact that Napoleon, having spent one night in the small but remarkable capital of Jamestown under the curious gaze of many inhabitants, chose to move up the valley and accept accommodation at The Briars. This was the home of a local family, where the summerhouse was adapted, whilst waiting for his intended 'internment' residence, Longwood House, to be prepared for him. Hence the eventual purchase of these properties by the French Government.

The silk experiment was a failure, but is still remembered today by 'China Lane' a short roadway leading towards The Briars.

Whilst these mementos have little or no connection with things that are of relevance historically (no disrespect to Napoleon, a hero of my school-days!) yet still they manage to make the most of their disadvantages, whilst those which were once of considerable importance, for various reasons, do not.

* * *

One place, nearer to home and coming under the latter 'umbrella', is Dieulacres Abbey, once a thriving Cistercian monastery on the outskirts of the Manor of Leek, in N. Staffordshire. Originally founded as a community of monks at Poulton on the River Dee, 5 miles south of Chester, in 1146, it offered prayers for the health and safety of Ranulph II, Earl of Chester.

It was Ranulph's son, Hugh Cyveliok, who enclosed large areas of forest in East Cheshire and, by tradition, died at Swythamley. He took a leading role in the Barons' wars waged against Henry II, even encouraging Brittany in northern France to rebel. However it was his successors who gave the monks (by then amalgamated with the Cistercians) lands and privileges in various parts of Cheshire, added to which several wealthy landowners contributed manors, a village and areas of rights of pasture.

The Cistercians, whose forte was sheep rearing and wool production, acquired pastures at Chelford and Withington near Macclesfield. When the monastery began to suffer from incursions by Welsh raiders, the then Earl, Ranulph de Blunderville, (inspired by a dream which took on legendary proportions), granted a large area of land around the township of Leek to the community on 22nd April 1214. Eventually they received the entire township of Leek and the abbey of Dieulacres was built.

The site already supported the Chapel of the Blessed Virgin Mary and a Hermits' cave close by comprising three cells (the latter still in existence today). A deed, circa 1240-57, confirms rents from a plot on Chestergate in Macclesfield to the Chapel of St. Mary, which suggests a connection, particularly as it was Blunderville who had granted the rights and privileges of a borough to Macclesfield.

By 1254 the abbey was well-established, having lands to the north including Swythamley; to the west and south, boundaries with Rudyard and the River Churnet, and on its eastern side lands almost equalling those on the west; in total at least 1,800 statute acres.

The monks had pigs, 200 head of cattle and a considerable number of sheep. The adjoining smaller Wincle Grange, which belonged to the Cistercians of Combermere, was allowed 2,000 sheep, but although not known, Dieulacres must have at least equalled this.

Inevitably disputes arose with neighbouring estates and their patrons, and the Black Death, as elsewhere, appears to have had a devastating effect. By the 1390s N. Staffordshire had become notorious for its lawlessness with the monks suffering badly; however, the abbey survived until 1538 – the time of Henry VIII and the dissolution of the monasteries.

Passing through many private hands, ownership meant destruction and the use of valuable stones for local building purposes, such as the Abbey Farm and Abbey Inn; today the only reminders of a once thriving abbey. Ironically, as late as the 1960s, there remained a few piers and parts of the foundation walls, resulting in the site being declared an Ancient Monument by the Ministry of Public Buildings and Works in 1964. This was to ensure 'a degree of protection from further acts of vandalism'. One can only comment, 'the road to Hades is paved with good intentions'.

Side view of the Abbey Inn built 1702, incorporating valuable stones from the nearby Abbey of Dieulacres.

The valley originally supporting Dieulacres Abbey. On the right is Abbey Farm, whilst off the right hand side of the photo, on the horizon, is the tower of St. Edward's. the Parish Church of Leek. To the left of the central tree lies, what remains of, the foundations of Dieulacres Abbey, now defined partially by a pile of old tyres.

Grammar school 500th Anniversary

The Queen's visit to the town on the 24th July 2002, incorporating King's School, has now become part of Macclesfield's history. Until the reign of the usurper Henry IV (begun 1399), the Royal links were strong and visits not infrequent, but with the advent of the House of Lancaster, things were never the same again.

Yet, by a quirk of fate, our present Queen does have a family connection with Macclesfield, for not only must we credit Charles Roe with the building of the first silk mill but also the attendance of one of the Queen's forefathers at what was then known as Macclesfield Free Grammar School, now King's School.

Having already mentioned the partnership between Charles Roe and Brian Hodgson in the copper and brass concern of Roe & Co. in my article to commemorate the Queen Mother's 100th birthday, (see pages 174-175) it is sufficient only to make the briefest mention here.

Without a share in the partnership it is doubtful whether or not Brian Hodgson, landlord of The Old Hall at Buxton, would have had any connection with Macclesfield. However, his eldest son, Robert, who also entered the business, lived for a time in the town until circa 1767, when he moved to Daisybank, Congleton. From there Robert supervised the work carried out in the rolling mills at Havannah, in the parish of Eaton. A subsequent move, presumably at the time of his marriage in 1772, saw the family residing in Moody Hall in the centre of

Congleton, where his first child Robert Jnr. was born and in due course consideration had to be given to his education.

Charles Roe came from a family keen to promote education, in fact some of his forefathers had been headmasters of grammar schools. Charles must have been delighted, therefore, when his elder sister, Mary, married the headmaster of the Macclesfield Free Grammar School, Rev. Rowland Atkinson.

The school reorganised in 1762, after which Rev. Atkinson was paid a salary of £100 per annum, making him the highest paid headmaster of any Cheshire grammar school. It was well endowed with lands and profits, thanks to the overseeing and gifts of those with successful commercial interests over the centuries. Appreciating the importance of education to suit a more modern world, Roe and Atkinson pushed for a more modern curriculum e.g. modern languages and geography, alongside the traditional classical studies.

There were private junior schools in the town for both boys and girls, whilst French was taught by private tuition in the premises of a French tutor on Mill Street. However, it was not until after Rowland's death in 1773 that an Act was proposed by the Governors for the purpose, which became law in 1774; yet the wheels turned slowly.

In 1788 an 'additional Master' was engaged for teaching reading, writing and arithmetic and the school gained an excellent reputation. The Napoleonic Wars intervened causing severe economic depression throughout the country, but although general legislation, freeing all grammar schools from their obligations to teach predominantly classical studies, was not passed until 1869, Macclesfield was well ahead.

An invoice, sent to the parent of a pupil for the term ending Midsum-

In the background behind the trees is the present day King's School, built 1910. The foreground (now part of Churchill Way) is the site on which stood the previous school building of 1748-1910, attended by Her Majesty's forefather Robert Hodgson, Jnr.

The school building of 1748-1910 on King Edward Street. I included a drawing of the school in my article on pages 44-45 (vol. I), but thanks to Les Kirkham of the Family History Society this excellent copy of an original engraving circa 1848 (? a centenary souvenir perhaps) has come to light and gives far more detail, including the interesting iron gates and, apparently, two or three of the pupils!

mer 1840, whilst showing expenses due in relation to 'Greek Grammar' 7/6d. (37p.) etc., also lists 'Butler's Geography' 9/- (45p.) and 'French Master' 10/6d. (52p.) together with 'Histoire de France' 4/6d. (22d.)

This particular pupil had attended a private school until the age of 12 years, when he then transferred to the Macclesfield Free Grammar School, exactly the same situation as the son of Robert Hodgson, Moody Hall, Congleton; but the latter had begun his three year course much earlier in 1785.

Robert Jnr., a gifted pupil, was admitted to Peterhouse College, Cambridge at only 15 years of age in 1788. His subsequent career is well documented, culminating in his preferments of Rector of St. George's, Hanover Square London and Dean of Carlisle. Rev. Robert's granddaughter, Francis Dora Smith, married the 13th Earl of Strathmore in 1853, and their granddaughter, Elizabeth, was our late, much admired, Queen Mother.

The present school building dates from 1910, but the one attended by young Robert, long demolished, stood on King Edward Street. It appears to have been used as a residence for the first Dissenting minister of the King Edward St. chapel, and was subsequently bought by Sir Peter Davenport, a retired army officer, knighted as a Collector of Taxes. After Sir Peter's death it was purchased for the school in 1748.

The original foundation was accepted by a Victorian historian as 1502, because Sir John Percyvale's will of January 1503, containing a bequest for the establishment of the school, appeared as 1502/3 under the old dating system. The subsequent death of Sir John and the building of the Savage Chapel (first 'home' of the school) saw the passage of a few months. But what are a few months in a lifetime, or more to the point, 500 years? It does nicely coincide with Her Majesty's Golden Jubilee.

Christ Church

A remarkable set of circumstances originally produced this article in August 2002.

About four weeks before I had bought two interesting and nicely framed copies of engravings from off one of the outdoor market stalls viz: 'The National School in Duke Street' (long demolished – the site of which is now part of a car park), and '19th century engraving of Christ Church School built in 1840'. Whilst the one of the National School is well-known, I had not previously seen the one of the Christ Church School, which I subsequently dated as circa 1870, but on further investigation decided on a slightly earlier date of 1865.

Only one week later, Julie Brinton, one of the 'guardians' of Christ Church, rang to say that the Museums' Director, Louanne Collins. had found an engraved stone slab in storage of some significance to Christ Church, and had it duly delivered to the church – I hurried to see it!

The story was that the stone had been retrieved from a builder's skip in the early 1980s (location unknown), by a lady who had subsequently made use of it in her garden as a paving stone. On her removal to Poynton, realising that it could be of historical interest, she had given it to the Silk Heritage Centre.

Everyone, like myself, thought that the school built by 1840 (actually 1839) had been the first building created as a school house outside the Christ Church building itself, yet, what remains of the inscription indicates that an earlier one existed from 1795. As the photograph clearly shows, the stone at some time has been reduced in size to fit into a convenient modern location; however, the question is 'Where had it been in situ originally?' My interpolations together with the existing script are reproduced below the photograph.

Thanks once more to Les Kirkham of the Family History Society who, some time ago, allowed me sight of the earliest property deed for the Christ Church school building of 1839; also Jim Magnall, caretaker of Christ Church (now administered by the Redundant Churches Commission), who provided a copy of a Charity Commission Report (printed February 1905); and a rare photo of the school on an Edwardian calendar, I have managed to piece together an interesting story.

Mary, daughter of Charles Roe, was living at Sutton Hall when she died unmarried on 18th August 1787 aged almost 32 years. Her will, prepared some two years earlier, provided many bequests, the most significance being a sum of £600 to be invested by trustees (viz: the then minister of Christ Church, Rev. David Simpson and church wardens) for the education of poor children in the area.

David Simpson began the school in Christ Church on Lady Day, 25th March 1790. In 1795 almost £197 was used to build a school, with a house adjoining for the master, which would have been built on Roe land close by the

Above left: Christ Church school photo as it appeared on an Edwardian calendar (year unknown). The house has been replaced by the playground. **Above right:** The engraved stone reads – This school and the House adjoining for the Use of the Head-Master were erected by the late Rev. D. Simpson circa A.D. 1795 from the Interest of a Legacy of Six Hundred Pounds left in trust for ever to the then Minister and Wardens of Christ Church Macclesfield by the late Miss Mary Roe's Will of 1787 for the Education of poor children in the Town and Neighbourhood.

Christ Church school circa 1865, showing what appears to be the master's house on the left of the engraving. Could that be the memorial stone placed high above the school entrance? (Apparently not from those who knew the school well at the time of demolition). The original print is of poor quality.

church. The buildings were completed by 1797 (presumably displaying the stone) and a Mr. Perry appointed master.

Rev. Simpson died in 1799; the next minister, Rev. Horne, with other trustees, invested in a London property on 17th November 1807. The house, on the corner of Little-Friday Street and Bread Street was near the Lord Mayor's new Mansion House and a little south of the Guildhall. Just as today the property soared in value, trebling to £1,810 by 1810.

Economic depression, due to the Napoleonic Wars, saw Mr. Perry agree to resign his post in 1818, allowing funds to be diverted to the National and Sunday schools; as recompense he was allowed to remain rent free in the house until his death in August 1824. The house was then let to Peter Lowe for 15 shillings a year, but by December 1829 he was in arrears. He agreed to teach 20 children in return for living rent free and the remittance of his arrears.

Unfortunately the minister at this period, Rev. John Steele, became 'mentally deranged'; went to live in Bristol with relatives early in 1839, but was paid his stipend until his death in 1876! At this time it would seem that a Rev. W.W. Dickinson of Suffolk, member of a family attending Christ Church, took over trusteeship of

Mary Roe's fund, although the acting curate was William Pollock. It was Dickinson who conveyed the plot of land on Great King Street, with the building or school 'now erected', on 4th February 1840 to eight trustees including Rev. Pollock and Christopher Shaw Roe (Mary's nephew).

This suggests that the old school had been on the same plot but demolished to make way for the new building, yet leaving the master's house standing as shown on the left of the 1865 engraving. By the time of the 1871 O.S. map the house had been pulled down to make way for the playground in the Edwardian photo. The memorial stone must have been kept somewhere on site and removed in the early 1980s when the building (used as the church hall from 1970 when Bollinbrook school was opened) was finally demolished to make way for new flats, appropriately named 'Simpson's Court'.

It also suggests that the London property had been sold to defrain the costs of the new building.

Historically the stone is important for it proves that Christ Church provided the earliest Charity School in the town. And the facts reveal the sacrifices and considerable dedication shown by some of those early teaching 'pioneers'. By the mid-Victorian period the Christ Church Day School accommodated 118 boys and 114 girls.

Hats

During August 2002 I was delighted to help create a little history for the future, whilst at the same time uncovering yet another facet of Man's incomparable desire to make his presence felt.

Everyday civilian wearing of hats went out of fashion with the last war, yet I sense a revival amongst the younger generation, albeit in the form of baseball or baker-boy type hats. My own passion has never wavered, and three of mine have been accepted as additions to the collection owned by the Museum of Hatting in Stockport. One 'a Sheepskin Cone' will be on display in the New Donations Case for the month of September. Along with the hats went additional information collated out of interest.

Historically it is difficult to distinguish between a cap and a hat. The former appears to infer female headgear, and the latter male! Quoting from the Oxford English Dictionary 'CAP' seems to be derived from a woman's cap or hood of a cloak; in other words caps were usually made of soft material without brims, although cylindrical hats without brims were worn by some Orientals. Hats implied significance e.g. a superior rank, office etc. which no doubt stems from the fact that they were more expensive to produce than caps.

Whilst throughout history men have worn hats, women have periodically resorted to elaborate hairstyles, dressing their hair in various ways which, out of necessity, encouraged the wearing of cloaks with large hoods.

The earliest surviving headgear is that of 'The Ice Man' found in the Otztal Alps on 19th September 1991 and scientifically proved to be about 5,200 years old. The cap, described as a 'blunted cone' sewn together from individual pieces of fur with what appears to be a 'chin-strap' (two leather straps with the loose ends knotted together), was actually found during the second archaeological examination of the

A young Italian aristocrat of the 15th century wearing a hat without brim.

site on 19th August 1992.

Headgear has obviously been used for centuries and made out of all manner of materials, but it was the establishment of Craft Guilds towards the end of the 11th century (the majority of which were connected with textiles) that encouraged the popularity of hats. Turbans, berets and cones were in fashion, but experimentation began with crowns of different shapes to which brims were added, and Lombardy became famous for the production of felt hats.

By the 15th century fantastic designs were being created for men, and whereas women's styles were simpler (many wearing bonnets) by the middle of the century even those had mushroomed into the most outlandish shapes, yet never achieved the flamboyancy of those sported by men.

16th century fashion was dominated by Spain. In 1557 Leonell Duckett, Governor of the Company of Mines Royal and a member of the Mercers' Company in London, together with a partner, took over the patent for the importation of felts and hats from Spain and Portugal. This was, of course, the period of the reign of Queen Mary married to Philip II of Spain. In 1555 Philip had inherited the sovereignty of Spain, Sicily, Milan, the Netherlands and Franche-Comté from his father. Milan was one of the main cities of Lombardy, so there is little doubt that the fashion for felt hats had spread throughout the Spanish domains from there, resulting in their exportation to England Several Macclesfield wills at this period contain items of Spanish 'sylk' buttons.

Strictly speaking hat making refers to the production of men's hats, whilst millinery relates to women's, and the latter is derived from a vendor of goods from Milan.

During the 17th century the French began to develop their own fashions, but hats changed little, they were mostly wide-brimmed with gold cord around the crown. The Civil Wars in England caused great disruption to commerce, and during the Parliamentarian Period many cottage industries appear to have been reorganised as land and properties were sequestrated. Like the button industry of the Macclesfield area, the production of hats around Stockport seems to have become well-established at this time.

And whilst Macclesfield never gained a reputation for hatting, yet it did support the trade by the presence of hatband makers in the town; one in particular, James Bower, built several cottages in 1770 in Charlotte Street, now part of the premises of the George and Dragon public house on Sunderland Street.

An historically important hat is that relating to the Garland Festival in Castleton, Derbyshire; part of the original costume worn after the Restoration of the Monarchy in 1660. It is on display in the museum collection which, from next year, will be housed in superb new premises; the significance – it was worn for the annual celebrations of Oak Apple day (29th May) during the period when Charles Roe's father, Rev. Thomas, was vicar of St. Edmund's, Castleton, and Charles would have seen it worn at the ceremony when a young boy.

An 18th century advertisement for a head covering to an elaborate hair style.

The author with items from her hat collection begun in the 1950s.

King Charles Spaniels

I recently bid farewell to a loyal and dear friend, Charlie, or, to give him his official title, 'Charles of Macclesfield Park', my thirteen and a half year old Blenheim, King Charles spaniel (apparently a good age for this particular breed).

Charlie aged II years in Macclesfield (South) Park, 2000.

This article, whilst predominantly featuring King Charles spaniels, is written for all those responsible dog owners, breeders and admirers who have suffered the same fate and with whom empathy is unavoidable.

The original Encyclopaedia Britannica, published in Edinburgh 1771, sets out a 'Genealogical Table of the different races of DOGS', and groups together 'the hound or beagle, the terrier, the braque or short-tailed settling dog' and the spaniel because 'they have the same form and the same instincts; and differ only to the length of their legs, and size of their ears, which in each of them are long, soft, and pendulous'.

King Charles I (whose reign ended so disastrously with his execution in January 1649) was a great lover of animals, but it was his son, Charles II, who was particularly fond of small spaniels, also known as toy-dogs or comforters, with their pug-noses and drooping ears. As a result, after the Restoration of the Monarchy in 1660 when Charles II returned to rule, the small spaniel came into vogue as a pet and consequently acquired its royal title for the breed.

But that was not the only honour it received, a law was passed allowing it to have total liberty to go where it liked and do what it liked without the owner being prosecuted. This law has never been repealed, although I am certain that owners of these remarkable spaniels (surprisingly considered sixth in order of efficient guard dogs) would not take undue advantage of their privileged circumstance.

No doubt Charles II had developed his admiration for the breed during his exile on the Continent, where they had been popular for at least 200 years. It is surprising how many paintings from the late 15th century onwards depict miniature spaniels: I often find them tucked away under tables, in corners and in the foreground of landscapes.

It is interesting to see that one of the earliest

English paintings to include small spaniels, is that of a hunting party during the reign of Henry VII (1485-1509). The forest scene comprises two huntsmen on foot, (the one on the right is blowing a horn); four large hounds and two tan-coloured small spaniels. The dogs are surrounding a wild boar which lies prostrate on the ground, pinned down by its assailants.

About the same period an Italian painting (see illustrated detail) suggests that the small dog with the unmistakable characteristics of a 'Blenheim', was treated as a pet; this one accompanies two formidable looking females and a parrot on a balcony.

By the Elizabethan period small spaniels had also reached the status of pets in England, clearly shown in a small portrait of a lady with her 'comforter', exhibited in the Bowes Museum, Barnard Castle.

Their privileged position in France is indicated by an excellent oil painting in the Louvre. The scene of 'A Ball at the Court of Henry III of France' (he died 1589 – the last of the Valois dukes to occupy the French throne) shows a ring of dancers accompanied by musicians, with onlookers grouped around. On the left is a benign looking greyhound, but in the extreme lower right-hand corner are two playful Blenheims, obviously enjoying their frolics on the dance floor.

Detail from an early 16th century Italian painting of a small (later known as a Blenheim) spaniel.

Adlington Hall, the 18th century home of Charles Legh, an avid breeder and admirer of King Charles spaniels.

Even the famous painter Pierre Auguste Renoir (1841-1919), who was in great demand to produce portraits of people after 1870, executed a delightful portrait of a tricolour King Charles which hangs amongst a superb collection of his works in the Smithsonian, Washington.

A local 18th century enthusiast and breeder of King Charles spaniels was Charles Legh of Adlington Hall. He was a great character, who inherited the estate at his father's death in 1739 when 42 years old. His Commonplace Books are full of his own poetry, notes on hymns and anthems, cures for ailments and other useful advice. I cannot resist repeating one of my favourites from the latter – 'To prevent being troubled with Gnats in Bed Lay Horse dung on ye Floor'!

His notes on 'my Little Spaniels' are a delight. Altogether 62 are listed by name, eight he kept 'at home' e.g. Black Fox and Chloe; four were given as presents (presumably to good friends – one such was Nancy given to Thomas Walker, who could have been the important Manchester merchant and associate of Charles Roe) and the remainder must have been sold – but every owner is accounted for. And he even commissioned a portrait of his favourite bitch with her puppies, which still hangs in the Hall for visitors to enjoy.

Pearlwall

In April 1999 I wrote an article featuring Margery Meadow (in existence for at least 500 years) and Worth Hall orchard, both of which adjoined the lower part of Chestergate, with what is now Pinfold Street on the western side and Catherine Street on the east.

This article also features a significant meadow, contemporary with the one called Margery, but this time in the Beech Lane and Coare Street area of the town. However, before introducing Pyrlewall (later Pearlwall), an interesting follow-up occurred from the original mention of Worth Hall.

* * *

Pearle Street today; the name is a reminder of the medieval meadow or field known as Pyrlewall.

The owner of 7 Catherine St., a Mr. Farr (who subsequently moved to the South Coast in 1999), offered his earliest deed, dated 25th March 1794, for perusal. At that date the plot of land was part of 'Churchfield' (an obvious reference to Christ Church) and owned by William Roe, Charles Roe's eldest son, who was then resident in Liverpool. William leased the plot to a joiner, Joseph Bloor, and gave permission for building to take place on the site. Thus began the development of Catherine Street named after William's elder sister.

Having read the article, Mr. Farr deduced that the north-west corner of his plot must have adjoined Worth Hall, and could possibly explain an interesting find he had made on the premises. He showed me a small enclosed patio at the rear of his property, which he had laid out. When digging in

Part of Coare Street built on the Pearl Walls field.

the north-west corner to create a small water feature, he had unearthed a very large column-like stone and deduced it was 'very old' because of certain features. It had obviously been created as a jamb which could have supported a large stone lintel in the manner of the standing stones at Stonehenge with their tenon and mortise features. The jamb also had the remains of some sort of fastening device on one side, suggesting it had been accompanied by a large gate or door.

Unfortunately the stone is no longer visible, having been incorporated into the base of the patio and water feature. However, Mr. Farr was convinced that it was part of a significant building which, at one time, had stood in the vicinity.

* * *

Whilst the earliest mention of Margery Meadow is in a deed of 1332, Pyrlewall is slightly earlier (1329), yet both in the reign of King Edward III who had ascended the throne in 1327.

Of course these meadows, so named, could have existed years earlier, but I suspect that Margery was relatively new, created out of an encroachment on the very edge of the 'King's Park', whereas Pyrlewall had been there for at least a century, possible two.

Today Pearle Street is our modern reminder, but, although the spelling had been corrupted to 'Pearl' by the 18th century, this is misleading.

The late Charlie Hadfield (retired chemist and local history fanatic) suggested that 'Pearle' represented purlieu, which was a piece of land on the edge of a forest, subject to Forest Laws, yet had become an area of common usage by local inhabitants, particularly for hunting and gaming.

This is a plausible explanation; however, the word pyrle, whilst later becoming 'purl' had another alternative – 'pirl', (it was never 'pearl(e)' this is a local adaptation) 'to pirl' meant to twist, wind, curl or create waves on a pond. As the name of the meadow from earliest times is 'Pyrlewall' or later 'Pearl walls' it seems to suggest a winding wall or walls enclosing the area.

Thanks to an offer by Mr. Ken Osborne, owner of a property on Coare St., allowing sight of his deeds, it is now possible to state that the field called 'Pearl Walls' occupied an area adjacent to Beech Lane; whilst other deeds additionally suggest that it ran from Cumberland Street to Northgate Avenue (the latter named after a medieval North Gate of the town which could have led out through the Pyrlewall).

The meadow was part of the Mydelfield (Middle field) of the borough in medieval times. From 1329 to about 1500 (Henry VII's reign) it was owned by various leading burgesses and mayors of the town from families such as Davenport, Rowe and de Macclesfield. By the early 1700s it was part of an estate owned by a solicitor of Nantwich, Samuel Harryman (the house is now known as Cumberland House on Jordangate – a doctors' surgery).

The estate was soon bought and occupied by a remarkable man, John Stafford, a lawyer who subsequently held both offices of Town Clerk and Clerk of the Manor and Forest of Macclesfield. He died in 1775 owning over 1,000 acres in the High Peak area and various other properties. The land surrounding his Jordangate home, and part of his Jordangate estate, was known by the various names of 'the Back street field' (Back Street is now King Edward Street), 'the pearl Walls and the pearl Walls meadow'; in all about 25 statute acres.

After John Stafford's death in 1775 the estate passed to his son, William (who only lived a few months) and daughters. By the early 19th century the field called 'the Pearl Walls' was owned by John Brocklehurst the Younger, silk manufacturer of Hurdsfield, who divided it up into plots for leasing from 1819, allowing Brock Street to be laid out and 'Beach' Street (Coare Street) leading from Beach (Beech) Lane. The demise of this meadow land was inevitable as houses mushroomed in order to accommodate an expanding population.

Cumberland House, Jordangate, which, in the 18th century, had a considerable area of land adjoining to the rear and north; part of this was the Pearl Walls field which extended to the present Northgate Avenue along the western side of Beech Lane.

Bells

On Sunday, 1st December 1745, members of the congregation attending morning service at St. Michael's chapel (now the Parish Church), far from being in a festive mood had other urgent matters on their minds.

Prince Charles Edward Stuart, son of 'James VIII of Scotland', was on his way south to claim the English throne for his father 'The Old Pretender', and, according to reports from local spies, was already entrenched in Stockport. But Bonnie Prince Charlie was determined not to tarry long, appreciating that an element of surprise was imperative, so he had rapidly pushed on with his Scottish rebel army.

What horror, consternation and amazement must have been felt locally when, half way through the church service, the Macclesfield parishioners had learnt of the approaching Scots and, as a consequence, had 'run out . . . in ye utmost Confusion'.

Before long, with bagpipes playing, the Regiments in Highland Dress marched up Jordangate. Fearing repercussions, an effort was made to give them 'a peal of ye Bells', but only four ringers could be found and 'they rung ye bells backward not with design but thro' Confusion', (this was according to a report by John Stafford, Clerk of the Manor & Forest of Macclesfield and the local representative of the Earl of Derby).

Mr. Ivor Nichols (former Head of Bollinbrook School) in his excellent history of the bells and ringers of St. Michael's, compiled in 1992, suggests that this 'backward' ringing of the peal of bells could have been a deliberate attempt to signal danger to the people in the surrounding area; or, due to an inexperienced ringer, could have created an out of sequence peal which sounded as though the bells were being rung in reverse order.

His researches reveal the first mention of the bells in 1549, when four are recorded in the tower; in 1701 two more were added making six in total, one of which was the 'little bell'.

On that fateful December day in 1745, with

The Russian Tzar Bell, created as the largest in the world (1733-35), demoted to a tourist attraction in the grounds of the Kremlin, Moscow.

228

The Whitechapel Bell Foundry of Mears & Stainbank who took over Rudhall's of Gloucester in 1844. This is the foundry responsible for the bells of Westminster Abbey. The only other bell foundry still in existence in England is Taylor's of Loughborough, which won the 19th century contract for St. Michael's bells, and is still used for the repairs, replacements etc. of the Macclesfield church bells.

the sonorous tones of bells?

The superb technology of the Ancient Chinese had brought the art of bell production to perfection by the time of the Chou dynasty (c. 1122-221 B.C.). Their bells, mostly created for temple use and often decorated, encouraged the manufacture of sets of miniature bells to be used as instruments in the creation of music.

Russian bell foundries did not come into existence until the 13th century. However, they can claim to have cast the largest bell in the world between 1733-35; known as the Tzar Bell, and weighing 180,000 kilograms (almost 179 tons!), it sits in the grounds of the Kremlin, but has never been rung due to a crack created by a fire of 1737.

six bells but only four ringers, the latter no doubt in a state of terror should later accusations of traitor be levelled against them, it is hardly surprising that their rhythm was upset. John Stafford, a lawyer of considerable repute, would certainly have acknowledged their efforts to ring a peal signalling danger had it been so. Perhaps recognising an incorrect peal he had assumed a sequence in reverse order. Whatever the intent (or not) behind the action it does signify the importance of bells in past decades.

They were used to warn of danger; encourage rejoicing; call people to worship; count out the hours or draw attention to significant events. Today they are very much an emblem of the Christmas Season together with the Christmas tree and Father Christmas. Usually depicted in silver or gold they add a touch of regality to the celebration of Christ's birth, appearing on Christmas cards; as ornaments on Christmas trees, or ringing out the call to church on Christmas Eve (as, of course, on other days during the year).

Bells have been with us from almost the time when Man discovered how to make bronze around 2,000 B.C. What better way to send out non-visible signals over a large area than with

Because of the ritual and mystique associated with bells, their manufacture is the only metallurgic process 'restricted to casting with alloys of a constant composition which varies little from the formula 78% copper to 22% tin'. Otherwise founders have always used their own formulae which are often kept secret. The usual recipe for bronze is approximately 90% copper to 10% tin.

Charles Roe intended the Christ Church tower (completed 1776) to house eight bells. The minister of St. Michael's, not to be outdone, gained support for also ordering eight bells from Thomas Rudhall of Gloucester. Charles immediately increased his to ten, which later caused many problems and the removal of two of them. However, both commissions were completed by the Rudhall foundry in 1777 but Christ Church was first.

Today the Roe church again has 10 bells, but St. Michael's 12, the latter augmented to 10 in 1835 and 12 in 1923. Visiting ringers come from far and wide to take up the challenge – more bells – more complicated peals to master. Hopefully the bells will long ring out their Christmas peals.

Eleanor's Chapel

Welcome to 2003 – yet many of us must be wondering what the year will bring. One very much overworked expression at the moment seems to be, 'We must move with the times'; but what does this mean? Ask any reasonable historian and they will tell you that history repeats itself every hundred years or so. Some people never seem happy unless they are changing things, but is it always for the best? The answer lies with succeeding generations.

A 13th century chapel in Southern Poland (once part of the Holy Roman Empire). Its outward appearance belies its beautiful and quite roomy interior. Queen Eleanor's chapel would have had a similar appearance.

True to form it is little more than 100 years since the last major restructuring of Macclesfield Parish Church, and now more is to come; but what originally caused 13th century Macclesfield 'to move with the times' and create a religious building on the site in the first place? The answer seems shrouded by the mists of time and is something of an enigma.

One hundred and fifty years had passed since the time of the Norman Conquest and, at last, Macclesfield was on the point of achieving its status as a borough.

With the prospect of a reliable source of income the then Earl of Chester, Ranulph, is credited with making a decision and allowing a borough to be established. This created freemen, otherwise known as aldermen and burgesses, who elected a leader to become mayor, and each paid his annual fee for his burgage. Not only did they gain the concession of trading free in the borough, but also elsewhere, especially within the City of Chester – a significant medieval port and important centre of guild activity.

Guilds were 'bodies of men banded together in sworn brotherhood' and some had been in existence in England long before the Norman Conquest.

The tomb effigy of Eleanor of Castile, reproduced by Courtesy of the Dean and Chapter of Westminster. She was an extremely intelligent, beautiful and religious woman who made a considerable contribution to the development of Macclesfield.

In the City of London there were sufficient members eventually to create individual guilds, whereas elsewhere the artisans and merchants tended to consolidate into one, which in many towns metamorphosized into corporations; as appears to have happened in Macclesfield. With a variety of commodities on offer in the markets of the small town, and the establishment of a vast trading network, Macclesfield was becoming affluent as the village changed into a township.

The local freemen would have made their way out through the North Gate of the town, across the townfields and river to the church of Prestbury (described as a 'church of some worth'), sometimes walking in procession to celebrate their Saint's day and other important festivals.

The church had been granted to the Abbey of St. Werburgh, Chester by Earl Hugh II (1154-89), a Cistercian foundation. Why then did Queen Eleanor (having received the Manor & Forest of Macclesfield as part of her dowry upon her marriage) petition for a chapel adjoining the borough, within such a comparatively

short distance of Prestbury church?

Her action goes some way towards confirming the enduring legend that, whilst visiting Macclesfield, Eleanor had had a vision which directed her to build a chapel on the rocky outcrop overlooking the river valley. Whilst some modern historians prefer to deal only in hard facts, it must be remembered that this was a period of religious fervour; an era of visionaries and miracles as evidenced by the lives of St. Agnes (of Montepulciano) and St. Bridget (of Sweden).

Eleanor had accompanied her husband, Edward, to the Holy Land on crusade, and I feel certain that she saw something in the landscape here which reminded her of that experience. The views along the road from Buxton to Macclesfield (A537) are reminiscent of those along a roadway in central Jordan; and the steep and rugged cliff-like hill, rising from Macclesfield manor, with its river flowing alongside a marshy bog below which was no doubt full of reeds, would have evoked memories of the rivers in the Holy Land.

It would have been necessary to petition the

Pope for permission to build the chapel, even a portable altar had to be sanctioned by the Holy Pontiff in Rome, but she succeeded; the chapel was built probably in the late summer of 1278 and formerly established by Letters Patent of Edward I on 25th January 1279.

The Chapel, dedicated to All Saints (also referred to as All Hallows) must have had special significance for the Queen, because she had been married on All Saints Day, 1st November 1254. In all 1,255 ancient English churches were given this dedication, only those of the Virgin Mary were more popular.

The consecration was performed by the Bishop of St. Asaph, a Dominican. He was a member of Eleanor's favourite Order of friars; its founder St. Dominic had been born in her father's province of Castile.

It is thanks, therefore to Eleanor of Castile's intervention that the freemen of Macclesfield and their families had their own chapel – and this was very important to them.

Borough

Although no one knows exactly when the borough was created, it has always been assumed that Randle (III) de Blundeville, Earl of Chester, granted the charter. He joined a crusade to Jerusalem in 1219 and was an important figure in the Egyptian campaign. On returning he is said to have created the boroughs of Chester, Stockport and Macclesfield, which suggests that he was granting privileges in return for the support he had received from his Cheshire yeomen.

Surprisingly, whilst Cheshire was famous for its dairy produce, including cheese, it was also renowned for fish, bred in its numerous lakes and meres, which were salted and dried. Macclesfield, with its position on the old salt routes running west to east, and a significant route from Scotland via the Lake District south (later chosen by Bonnie Prince Charlie in his attempt to gain the throne for his father in 1745), had become an ideal centre for the intermingling of itinerant merchants; so it had grown

A superb Victorian watercolour of the Macclesfield chapel (much enlarged in the 18th &19th centuries and now the Parish Church in the Market Place) circa 1413, said to be copied from an ancient drawing.

into an important and affluent market centre.

The Earl, in allowing the establishment of a borough, had also assured himself of a reliable source of income, as each freeman (otherwise known as a burgess but sometimes elected to the important position of alderman)) paid an annual fee for his burgage (today represented by the portion of rates paid by Macclesfield property owners to Cheshire County Council via the Corporation). This ensured that the freemen of Macclesfield not only gained the concession of trading free within the borough but also elsewhere, especially in Chester, a significant port and important centre of guild activity (as previously last month).

Guilds

Guilds, in existence in England long before the Norman Conquest, had been created for various reasons. Some had been founded for religious or charitable purposes, whilst others brought together tradesmen and artisans with similar interests as a form of insurance against violence, robbery, intimidation etc. But all had a patron saint, and their annual donations were utilised in a variety of activities, not least the maintenance of an altar and prayer ritual in their local church or chapel.

After 50 years of attending the church of Prestbury, now the Corporation had a focal point within the community, evidenced by the construction of an altar to 'The Virgin Mary' at which prayers were said for 'all the brethren and sisters of Our Lady Service'. This was typical of the altars maintained by guilds throughout the country.

The Chapel Building

With the building of the chapel the premier townsmen of Macclesfield could be buried locally instead of Prestbury, and also their children could be baptised more easily – an important consideration, particularly in the depths of winter. The people of Bosley had petitioned the Pope for many years before they were allowed their own chapel, otherwise they too, as many in the surrounding communities, had to make the arduous journey all the way to Prestbury.

Whilst the exterior of the chapel appears to have altered little until the 15th century, internally different altars at different times received their consecrations (as discussed in earlier articles). However, at the time of John de Macclesfield's connections with the town there is a reference in a deed of 1414 to a new chapel, which has previously been assumed to refer to a chapel incorporated into his new crenellated mansion near the King's highway (now Mill Street). However, there is no trace of such a sanction by the Pope and seems to infer an enlargement of Queen Eleanor's chapel when the tower and spire were added.

A Victorian watercolour 'from an Antient (sic) Drawing' of the chapel, which seems to identify with a representation appearing on an 18th century seal used by the Rural Deans of Macclesfield, must relate to that time. Shortly afterwards, in 1422, the Legh chapel was added on the southern side supposedly to receive the body of Sir Piers Legh who had died in France 1422. This has been disputed, for a mound in Lyme Park, known as Knight's Low, has been claimed as the burial site, though some believe this to be prehistoric in creation.

At the time of the reconstruction of Queen Eleanor's chapel early in the 15th century, many of the premier freemen of the borough, involved with the scheme, ensured their place in history for centuries to come by displaying their coats of arms on the tower. And there they have remained to this day.

Family Coats of Arms on St. Michael's Tower

Although emblematic devices had been used for centuries to represent tribes, families, towns and so forth, it wasn't until the reign of Edward I that English coats of arms were first regulated with the king's appointment of two heralds. However, it was Henry V (1387-1422) who was the great patron of heraldry. He created the post of Garter King of Arms by which a proclamation, forbidding the bearing of arms by anyone unless granted by the king or his heralds, was made.

The parish church of St Michael and All Angels with several of the coat of arms still visable on the tower.

234

It is interesting to note that the emblems, incorporated into the stonework of the Parish Church clocktower, appear to have been added about that time, for Henry V was crowned in 1413 when 26 years of age. So the affluent knights of Macclesfield, or their progeny, would have paid their fees to claim and display their symbols of nobility.

The earliest coats of arms are quite plain; a simple device on a shield, as evidenced by the emblematic accoutrements added to the outside of the tower where, of course, they were in full view of everyone entering the market place.

The Legh Family

One of the families claiming seniority in local affairs was that of the Leghs. The family pedigree claims descent from Gilbert de Venables, who accompanied William the Conqueror across the Channel and was knighted by him in 1066 on the battlefield of Hastings. As a consequence Gilbert received grants which included possessions in Cheshire. By 1086 he was one of the eight barons of the Palatinate of Chester, placed in authority by the king to oversee county affairs. One of his direct descendants married the daughter and heiress of Richard de

Brass rubbing of the remaining half of the Perkin-a-Legh brass in the Parish Church: courtesy of the Trustees of the British Museum.

The Legh Family coat of arms.

II) on the French campaigns. The Cheshire contingent of archers fought gallantly in the battle for Poitiers in 1356, a town situated 140 miles to the north-east of Bordeaux in Western France. The French chronicler, Froissart, wrote: 'If the truth must be told, the English archers were a huge asset to their side and a terror to the French; their shooting was so heavy and accurate that the French did not know where to turn to avoid their arrows. So the English kept advancing and slowly gaining ground'.

This was a great victory for the Black Prince whose men were said to total only 8,000, including 400 archers, whilst the French fielded 50,000!

Three years later Robert was described as one of the Black Prince's esquires and leader of the Macclesfield hundred archers. However, it was his son, Robert, who was knighted in 1386 and would have obtained confirmation of the Legh coat of arms.

Legh of High Legh; but their son, John, took the name of his birthplace and was known as John de Legh.

The Leghs became established at Adlington in 1315 because of a marriage with the family of de Corona who had been granted the small estate (later to be enlarged) by Henry III (father of Edward I).

Robert de Legh (1308-70) was a 'Riding-Forester' in the forest of Macclesfield and bail-iff of the hundred, and it was his son, Peter, who became the first Legh of Lyme (Hall).

Peter or, to give him his fashionable French name, Piers was given the important post of command at Chester Castle by Richard II – but unfortunately his loyalty to Richard cost him his life; he was beheaded by the usurper, Henry of Bolingbroke, in 1399. Henry, son of John of Gaunt, was soon to become Henry IV. It is believed that the body was brought back for burial locally, although at this time it is more than likely that Piers was interred in the Mother Church of Prestbury.

Piers's brother Robert of Adlington, had accompanied the Black Prince (father of Richard

Medieval warfare – England V France. It gave opportunities to local families such as the Leghs to win their spurs (an expression coined by Edward III when speaking of the Black Prince at Crécy 1346)

The device adopted was that of a unicorn's head; the unicorn represented purity and knightly honour yet was more favoured in Scotland at that time, which suggests Robert had distinguished himself in the Scottish campaign of the previous year.

Now Sir Robert, he took part in Richard II's Irish campaign of 1394, but after his uncle's execution in Chester he conveniently changed his allegiance to Henry of Bolingbroke. He died in 1408, so it fell to his son, yet another Robert, to ensure the family coat of arms was flaunted in Macclesfield market place – just in time – for the young man fell ill in France and died shortly before the Battle of Agincourt in 1415.

His cousin, Piers of Lyme, did take part in the battle, was knighted on the field, but later died in Paris in 1422 from a wound received in the siege of Meaux. His body was brought to Macclesfield for burial where the Legh chapel was created as a memorial together with the Perkin-a-Legh brass.

The Macclesfield Family

Piers Legh of Lyme was a contemporary of John de Macclesfield and, by a turn of fate, they died in the same year, 1422. Accompanying the Legh coats of arms on the church tower, amongst others is that of the Macclesfield family.

John had schemed and worked long and hard to establish a dynasty, and there is little doubt that his original intention was to consolidate his land acquisitions into a large estate in Macclesfield lying to the south of the Market Place.

At the time of his death, although he had relinquished his rights for the sake of the family, the estate potentially stretched from the upper eastern side of what is now Mill St. (i.e. from Queen Victoria St. to the Market Place), down the hill to the River Bollin and Hurdsfield. His former properties, flanking the southern side of the Market Place, had underground taverns represented today by the large cellars under the present buildings, particularly that of Cottrill's.

Recent redevelopment of the site has produced some interesting finds. Unfortunately the first one, a large brown earthenware jar, had been smashed into small pieces by excavating machinery and the workmen, thinking it of no value, had consigned it to the rubbish dump before my arrival on site.

The description given was comparable to that of a Bellarmine, a large drinking jug with a

The Macclesfield Family coat of arms.

round 'capacious belly' and narrow neck. It was produced by the Protestant potters of the Netherlands to ridicule their antagonist, a Jesuit, Cardinal Bellarmine (1542-1621), and mostly used for ale. Perhaps the Macclesfield vessel had been similarly employed.

I was able to retrieve four further finds which include a piece from the base of a heavily potted brown-glazed earthenware container, reminiscent of the saggers into which pottery is placed in the kiln for firing, but it was probably a storage vessel in which victuals could be kept cool.

The most likely place of manufacture for these two brown earthenware items was Derbyshire. Derbyshire stoneware had been made for centuries (one of the earliest records relates to 98 AD) in an area covering the eastern side of the county. The pots were glazed in fascinating glassy hues of light to dark brown, dependant upon the minerals contained within the clay e.g. iron. The wares were mostly utilitarian items such as open and covered jars, stone bottles, stew pots, jugs of all shapes and sizes and so forth; in other words kitchen wares, appropriate at their particular period of manufacture.

The row, known as the Root Market at the time of the Napoleonic Wars, now with Cottrill's in the central position, is a very early site on which John de Macclesfield owned properties.

And as the Cheshire salt was transported into Derbyshire, there is little doubt that the wares completed the reverse journeys along the ancient packhorse trails.

* * *

Other discoveries, from the excavation of the large cellars and equally as significant, included a lovely shard from a large bright orange slipware plate. The design had been effected by trailing a pale yellow ochre slip (that is a mixture of clay materials in water in order to create a thick paste) across the surface. The pattern seems to represent a simple floral design of petals surrounding stamens and most probably it would have sported a geometric border pattern around the rim.

My articles on pages 102-105 (vol. I) reported the excavated archaeological finds on Manchester airport's runway 2 site and featured shards from a similar plate. Full details of manufacture were included with the suggestion of a Staffordshire origin. The additional find in Macclesfield further affirms my then comment 'These are fine examples of the types of pottery used by the residents of the Macclesfield area c. 1650-1750'.

The fourth item from the Market Place, a small brownish-yellow glass bottle complete with stopper, appears to be a 19th century medicine bottle. It is interesting to note that in the early 19th century William Lowe, the Borough druggist, occupied one of the properties on the row then known as the Root Market.

The final item, identified by a local vet as a pig's jawbone, was found three feet below ground level at the rear of the premises – a possible indication of an early middingstead (midden). It is an appropriate find as it allows mention of John de Macclesfield's connection with pigs.

* * *

Late in his career John became warden of St. Ant(h)ony's, a very wealthy hospice in Pig Street London. The Order of St. Antony's had been founded about 1100 AD, although Antony (251-356AD) had lived some 800 years earlier (if his dates are to be believed!). He was an abbott and hermit of Upper Egypt who spent time in Alexandria. Amongst some extant correspondence is a letter from the Emperor Constantine who, like many, considered him to be a great philosopher.

Items discovered by workmen during recent internal excavations of the business premises No. 35 Market Place. A brown shard, a pig's jawbone of unknown date, a 19th century medicine bottle and a 17th century shard from a large plate.

His Order of hospitallers treated many sufferers of ergotism (St, Antony's Fire); a condition caused by poisoning from eating diseased rye and other cereals. The hospitallers, to attract alms, walked the streets ringing bells, which were later hung around the necks of animals to protect them from disease.

Surprisingly an additional privilege was granted to their pigs; they were allowed to roam the streets, presumably recognisable by their tinkling collar-like accoutrements – and hence the name Pig Street adopted in London. Pigs and bells therefore came to feature strongly in St. Ant(h)ony's iconography.

* * *

Before leaving the market place it is important to confirm another find, though of a different nature.

The late Charlie Hadfield, whose family members have been chemists and apothecaries in Macclesfield for at least two hundred years, always insisted that his original premises, in the south-west corner of the market place, had an underground passage leading across the top of Mill Street to another property on the other side of the street. The passage or tunnel led from his cellar, but had been blocked off at some time earlier. His shop was in a prominent position being the first on the left hand side of the mall leading into the indoor market area from the Market Place, accompanied by what is now the shop of H. Samuel, jewellers on the right hand side of the mall.

Workmen, carrying out recent alterations in the cellars of the shop 5 Mill St., found an underground passage leading under the road towards the former premises of Charlie Hadfield. They came to what they said was 'a dead end', not realising that the passage had already been sealed off from the western end. They were told to seal off their part of the tunnel, but the mystery as to its original purpose and age remains.

The Rowe Family

Having already featured the Leghs of Lyme, Adlington and the Ridge, and also the Macclesfields – all prominent local families in the early history of the borough, whose coats of arms were incorporated into the stonework of the Parochial Chapel (now the Parish Church), it is now the turn of the Rowes (not to be confused with Charles Roe's family).

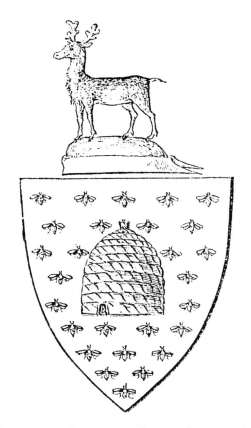

The Rowe Family crest granted 20 March 1653-4, this was however declared 'null and void' by Charles II in 1660. The early arms had varied, one with three bee-hives, others with different numbers of bees.

The first intimation of the Rowe family in the Macclesfield 'arena' is a record of Richard del Rowe (Row) as mayor for the year 1365-66, during the reign of Edward III. This was a stark period of English history due to the plague epidemic: The 'Pestilence', which literally decimated the population (i.e. one in ten) for each of the four years 1348-49, 1360 and 1379, left little more than half the population surviving.

Richard del Rowe obviously 'weathered the storms' for he also held the mayoral office for two further periods 1368-76 and 1378-88; in all a total of 19 years. Remarkably this was the beginning of a family tradition which provided burgesses, aldermen and mayors for a time span of some 320 years, far more than any other family in the Macclesfield area.

Richard, like his contemporary John de Macclesfield and many more, had grasped the opportunity to fill an important role in the community left vacant by the ravages of the Black Death. The Rowes contracted important

marriages with other knightly families close by, which included Downes of Taxal or Pott Shrigley, Fitton of Gawsworth and Worth of Tytherington, all of whom laid claim to coats of arms which found prominence on the tower of the Parochial Chapel.

And the Rowes also appreciated that dynasties were cemented by good education. One family member, Bryan Rowe, was educated at Eton from where, on 26th May 1499, he was admitted to King's College, Cambridge.

Eton had been founded in 1440 by Henry VI, reputedly for poor scholars, and competition for places must have been intense. Henry also founded King's College Chapel on 25th July 1446 from which the college rapidly developed. These foundations were subject to the king's patronage for the rest of his life and soon became 'major centres of learning'.

Bryan Rowe gained a Degree of Batchelor in Divinity and because of his excellent Scholarship 'was appointed to dispute before Henry 7th' when the king visited the college. Honours continued; a Fellowship then Vice-Provost of King's, but he unfortunately died in 1521 when he could not have reached 40 years of age; he is buried in the college chapel.

In Bryan's short and remarkable career he gained a reputation for his writings: A speech made to Cardinal Worlsey in 1520, on the pontiff's visit to the university, still survives, as do most items of his superb library of 101 titles in 116 volumes. A study of the collection has revealed that many of the books came via the Paris book-trade; some older ones are judged to be from Italy whilst others suggest a Rhine Valley origin, in particular Basle and Strasbourg. Very few were printed in England, but some came from the presses of T. Martinus in Antwerp and Louvain.

The inventory with his will is mostly taken up with his books; his personal items were few. Apart from bedding (2 bolsters, pillows, sheets etc.) his room was furnished with two old carpets, a cupboard with shelf, a chest, desk, three chairs, two mats and little more. He had few clothes comprising gowns (short and long); a jerkin; a jacket; a pair of red hose (very fashionable); a hat, a choir hood lined with silk and a riding hood, boots and spurs. He also possessed a surplice, candlesticks and three coloured images, accoutrements relating to his religious position.

By the time of the Civil Wars, the Rowes supported Parliament. Samuel, a Fellow of

Eton College founded in 1440 by Henry VI from where Bryan Rowe 'a native of Macclesfield' was admitted to King's College, Cambridge in May 1499.

King's College, Cambridge: Bryan Rowe became Fellow then Vice-Provost of the college in the early 16th century.

Gray's Inn claimed his coat of arms on 20th March 1653 as 'carved in stone upon the steeple of Macclesfield (sic) at ye foundation thereof which is there to bee seen this day'. This was a beehive beset with 10 bees, however earlier, in 1566, the family had claimed three hives beset with bees but this had been reduced to one by 1580.

Samuel died without an heir and his brother, William, an alderman in Berkshire, continued the line of descent.

Incidentally the Rowe Music Library at King's is named after a 20th Century man, Louis Thompson Rowe, which suggests another candidate for the family tree.

The Downes Family

In order to become a burgess, i.e. a person allowed municipal rights as a freeman of a borough, it was essential to hold a burgage, which was either land or other property from the lord of the borough. And for the early inhabitants of the area the lord of the Macclesfield borough was the Earl of Chester.

The original confines of the 13th century borough were very small. They appear to have been within a perimeter stretching along what is today Chestergate to Churchill Way; down the latter almost to Exchange Street; then curving eastwards to join Mill Street, and finally running north up Mill Street to include the western part of the market place. Where the town cross stood, close to the corner now occupied by the Natwest Bank.

By the time the enlarged chapel had been completed circa 1415, with its tower and el-

The Downes family coat of arms. The version in stone on the west side of the Parish Church tower is less ornate, as most early arms were.

egant spire, the borough boundaries had already begun their surreptitious expansion.

The families with the most influence and wealth, such as the Leghs, had estates out of town but, of course, in order to retain such status they were freemen holding burgages within the borough boundaries. And as already seen, those claiming superiority over the rest went to the expense of having their coats of arms displayed on the newly erected tower (and one or two also within the parochial chapel).

Whilst the Leghs, Macclesfields and Rowes dominated local affairs, a lesser-known family on the outskirts of the town were the Downes of Shrigley represented by an interesting shield. It is quartered (i.e. divided in four) with a buck in the upper left and lower right quarters, accompanied by a half leg in chain armour (referred to as couped below the knee) in each of the two remaining quarters.

The buck was granted to the Downes family; the earliest trace in the area is Robert de Downes of Sutton Downes in King John's reign (1199-1216). The Macclesfield mills were in Sutton Downes, today the area of Mill Green and stretching along Old Mill Lane and London Road to the Moss.

In 1345-56 Robert's descendant William de Dounes acquired a plot of land next to the mills' pond, between his own land and the buck-stall, which was a large net for catching deer. This is probably why the buck was adopted for the arms, signifying that part of the duties of the Downes' forestership.

The name Downes, also Dounes or Done, is recorded as coming from the Gaelic name 'O'Dubhain' and many Downes family members were living in Limerick and Tipperary in 1172.

In 1185 the future King John was sent to Ireland by his father on a conciliatory mission with the title 'Lord of Ireland', but the trip was a fiasco. The Irish chieftains, gathering to meet John and his entourage, rebelled when ridiculed by the royal party resulting in anarchy and bloodshed in many parts of Ireland. It does seem possible that Robert de Downes moved to England at this time to take up the prestigious position in Macclesfield Forest. As the Sutton family had jurisdiction in that area it was known as Sutton, which suggests that the part coming under Robert's control became known as Sutton Downes.

His descendants also acquired Taxal; another

A drawing of Shrigley Hall by the author based on a painting by William Turner. Shrigley Hall was demolished in 1820 in order to build Turner's fine 'modern' mansion.

Robert de Downes is listed as one of eight hereditary foresters in 1288 responsible for Taxal and Downes, and this forestership remained within the family until the death of a John Downes in 1621.

In 1313 Robert's second son William purchased lands in Shrygglelegh (Shrigley) adding the half legs to their shield, a possible pun for 'shrunken leg', to distinguish his line of the family. Another William succeeded his father and leased the Macclesfield mills, but it was this second William's grandson, Robert, who married an heiress, increased his land holding to include Upton and Worth and as owner of at least three burgages in the town saw the family coat of arms displayed in the stonework of the chapel.

Shrigley eventually united with Pott but the family remained at Shrigley Hall. Today the lovely church of Pott Shrigley is testament to their devotions. Robert's son Geoffrey, born circa 1447, a lawyer and fellow of Queen's college, Cambridge (1490-94) together with the college's benefactress, Lady Joan Inglethorpe, extended the chapel, adding the present tower with three bells and the dedication to St. Christopher. Geoffrey organised a small lending library and,

together with his patroness, formed a 'Brotherhood' with fees charged according to wealth; the poor were free.

The 18th century witnessed John Stafford, lawyer and town clerk, walking with his wife, her sisters and many more females to the safety of his friend Mr. Downes' house in Shrigley at the advent of Bonnie Prince Charlie's arrival in town. Suddenly three Highlanders arrived to search for guns having been informed Downes had three cases of pistols. Downes had three cases, one of which he had lent to a neighbour. John Stafford returned to Macclesfield to superintend matters but wrote of the incident 'those villains could not come to the knowledge of these things but through greater villains'.

Unfortunately the Downes family, like so many more in the late 18th century, had accrued considerable debts and the estate was sold in 1819 to a William Turner M.P. for Blackburn.

The Swet(t)enham Family

Another family involved in the early history of Macclesfield is that of Swetenham. However, unlike others, they are something of an illusive family. They hold the distinction of not only seeing their shield, bearing their simplified coat of arms, displayed in stone on the tower of what is now Macclesfield Parish Church from circa 1414, but from 1841 also on the tower of Pugin's Roman Catholic Church of St. Alban's on Chester Road.

It is important to remember that early coats of arms were simple affairs, displayed on the shields of knights and easily recognisable by their entourages. They were obviously easier to reproduce in stone, but later centuries witnessed additions and embellishments, ideal for display in the great halls to impress important visitors.

The family name of Swetenham is automatically associated with the parish of the same name, which was situated in the hundred of Northwich for administrative purposes. But the main branch of the family first appears in the neighbouring Somerford Booths, which was in the Macclesfield hundred.

Somerford Booths

Domesday lists Somreford (sic) representing farms at Somerford comprising the Hall and Park and also Somerford Booths Hall; Swetenham is not included.

The ancestor, Elias de Swetenham is recorded in the time of Richard I (1189-99) and apparently survived into the reign of Henry III, which

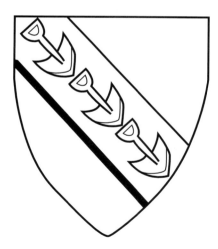

Above: The Swetenham coat of arms. The bend (i.e. diagonal band) displaying the three spades or shovels was originally sable (black), but changed to vert (green) by the Swetenhams of Somerford Booths. It is probable that the shields on the Parish Church were originally coloured but because of weathering have not only lost their colours but also some of the details.

began in 1216. From him are descended two distinct lines, the senior remaining at Somerford Booths (later known as Somerford juxta Marton) and a junior branch who created Swetenham Hall and are prevalent in Swetenham parish records from early in the reign of Edward I (1227-77).

Elias is interesting because he granted (leased) to Thomas de Macclesfield, Queen Eleanor's forest bailiff, his lands in Swetenham including an island called Rouhelegh. The rent benefited the knights of St. John of Jerusalem and was 12 pence per annum.

About that time, because of a marriage settlement, William Swetenham, great grandson of Elias, was given lands in Somerford by the Somerford family; these were of course in the Macclesfield hundred. This branch eventually acquired a considerable estate including burgages in Macclesfield borough. This indicates that the shield displaying the three shovels or spades of the Swetenham family on the parish church tower is that of the Somerford Booths family and not the Swetenham line.

Surprisingly it was not until 1613-19 that a William Swetenham of Swetenham is listed as mayor of Macclesfield. He might have been the first family member to hold the office, but not to be outdone he was shortly followed by another William Swetenham in 1625-26, who ensured that his entry was accompanied by Esquire (of Somerford Booths), emphatically declaring the seniority of his family line. No more Swetenhams have ever held the office.

An interesting development occurred in the late 17th century. Over the centuries a branch of the Davenport family had acquired large holdings in the Somerford area, and from time to time there were exchanges between the two families. However, the Davenports faired better than the Swetenhams, and the latter lost their connections with the parish. This seems to have coincided with the period of the Civil Wars, suggesting loyalty to the Crown and possible sequestration of their estates in lieu of paying a large fine to the Parliamentarians.

Swetenham Manor

After the Restoration, on 14th August 1665 Thomas Swetenham married the daughter of Sir Thomas Stanley of Alderley and decided to purchase Swetenham manor back from the Davenports. His only problem was lack of capital, so he approached his distant relative Edmund of

A rare 18th century engraving of Dallam Tower near Milnthorpe on the southern edge of the Lake District, home of Elizabeth Wilson, whose marriage to Phillip Swetenham ensured that his father's considerable estate in the Congleton and Macclesfield areas was included in the marriage settlement.

Somerford who lent him the money. Edmund in effect became the owner and is shown on property deeds as guarantor with Thomas Swetenham and Edward Davenport as tenants.

The estate was considerable comprising Swetenham Hall, 27 houses and lands, a dovehouse, a water corn mill, 20 gardens, 20 acres of land, 40 acres of meadow, 100 acres of pasture, 20 acres of arable, 60 acres of heath and furze (gorse), 20 acres of moor, 20 acres of land covered by water and other properties in Somerford Booths, Somerford juxta Brereton, Congleton, Swetenham including burgages in Macclesfield.

To date I have located three of the burgages in Macclesfield Town. Two of the properties were the subject of my article on pages 60-61 (vol. I) and occupied No.100 Mill Street (the former Pig & Whistle public house), though it seems probable that only one existed earlier on the site and was later divided.

The second burgage occupied the site of the new Macclesfield library on the corner of Jordangate and Brunswick Street, and the other on Back Street (now King Edward Street).

* * *

Before continuing the mini-saga of the Swetenham family I must point out that the variant spelling, Swettenham, is today in use, and appears to have been adopted permanently at some time in the 18th century. I have used the spelling appropriate to the period.

By the late 17th century Edmund Swetenham of Somerford Booths had ensured that his senior branch of the family had regained its stratum in society. His large loan to Thomas Swetenham, to provide the recovery of the Swetenham estate for the family, enabled him to negotiate an important marriage for his son, Phillip.

The whole of the estate, already detailed, was used to invest in the marriage settlement concluded on 30th April 1672. The bride-to-be was Elizabeth Wilson, eldest daughter of Edward Wilson Esquire, owner of Dallam Tower, a large estate in County Westmorland near Milnthorpe on the southern edge of the Lake District.

Edmund already had important contacts within the county of Cheshire as affirmed by the fact that one of his trustees was Sir Geoffrey Shakerley, knight and M.P. for Chester.

Unfortunately Phillip, a minor of 19 years at the time of his marriage, died the following

Above: The entrance to the Macclesfield library (former District Bank building). This property now stands on the site of one of the former burgages owned by the Swetenham family of Somerford Booths.

The tower of St. Alban's R.C. Church: the figure of St. Thomas of Canterbury is on the left with the Swettenham coat of arms beneath, and St. Winifrede of Wales on the right.

year, just two years before his father; but he had produced a son, Edmund, who, as an adult, became sheriff of Cheshire.

It is interesting to note that the general opinion (including that of the early 19th century historian Ormerod) seemed to conclude and credit Thomas Swetenham with the ownership of the family estate, including Swettenham Hall, an impression which Thomas had no doubt encouraged.

The situation appears to have given Thomas's family the opportunity of also negotiating important marriages for the offspring, who eventually seem to have managed the redemption of their debts and settled at Swettenham Hall.

The great grandson of Thomas, born 5th October, 1804 and named after him, married a Roman Catholic, Anna Maria. She was the daughter of Lieut-Colonel Luke Allen C.B. of the 90th Regiment of Dublin. They were married in 1829 but had no children.

St. Alban's R. C. Church

Anna Maria was a staunch Roman Catholic, but it seems unlikely that her husband ever converted to the church of her faith. Thomas's uncle was for a time Church of England minister of Swettenham church before accepting a post in Wales. Nevertheless Thomas does not seem to have discouraged his wife in her endeavours to promote the Roman Catholic cause.

Macclesfield was about to witness the building of its first Roman Catholic church since the Reformation, much to the delight of a congregation who had for many years worshipped firstly in premises at Sutton and then Mill Street, Macclesfield.

The Earl of Shrewsbury was an important patron in the Shrewsbury Diocese and was instrumental in promoting Pugin's abilities as an architect for the proposed building. He was also a generous benefactor to the project. As a consequence when the church tower was completed his coat of arms was given prominence.

In all, four imposing statues of saints were placed in niches in the tower. The two lower ones are those of St. Catherine holding a broken wheel on the eastern corner, accompanied by St. John the Evangelist, quill in hand and writing in a book, on the western corner. Those of St. Thomas of Canterbury, holding his shiny gilt crozier, and St. Winifrede of Wales, bearing a palm branch, are high up on the front of the tower. Beneath each is an angel holding a shield as a breastplate. Two of the shields are unrecorded, in fact one is blank, but the one beneath St. John represents the Shrewsbury coat of arms in memory of John, 16th Earl, who was so much involved with the enterprise.

The accounts show that Anna Maria Swettenham gave £100 to the building fund, a large sum in 1839. And there is little doubt that through her Irish and Dublin connections she rallied great support for the endeavour. This must be the reason why the angel beneath St. Thomas's feet is the one holding the shield sporting the Swettenham coat of arms: somewhat elaborated from that of St. Michael's parish church for it carries the bend on which the three spades or shovels appear.

Her husband, Thomas died on 12th November, 1861 leaving no children and it is probable that during the widowhood of Anna Maria the small but delightful Roman Catholic chapel was built adjoining Swettenham Hall for those of the faith in Congleton. Anna Maria lived out her days in Swettenham and was buried there in 1876.

Both lines of the Swet(t)enham family eventually descended through husbands of heiresses who assumed the name Swettenham and arms for their heirs: yet their descendants are now dispersed, leaving another void in relation to a family who had been caught up in local affairs for centuries.

Fitton Family

The Fitton family of Gawsworth is a family often referred to because of the speculation that Mary Fitton was the 'Dark Lady' of Shakespeare's sonnets (although a recent television programme suggests that it was a London Jewess with whom Shakespeare had an affair), and yet one which has been somewhat buried in the shadows.

The Anglo-Saxon chronicles relate that a Bishop Phytwine was consecrated as bishop of Whithorn at Elvet (now part of Durham City) circa 765. This was an important religious centre. St. Ninian's church and its priory are reputed to be the earliest Christian establishment in Scotland, the ruins of which now form an important site 12 miles south of Wigtown on the southeastern tip of the peninsula.

In the 9th century a fire destroyed the church and the area came under Viking rule. The name Phyton or Phytun is recorded after the Norman Conquest in Leicestershire, which suggests a variant of Phytwine and the likelihood that the family were English, having been settled here for centuries and, therefore, not part of William the Conqueror's contingent. It also suggests that they were devout Christians who had status under Anglo-Saxon rule and, like many more, would have quietly proved their allegiance to the new regime in order to regain prominence in society.

The land in Shawell, Leicestershire, was held in return for knight's service to the Earls of Chester and only 12 miles east of the rich monastery of Coventry, the pre-eminent bishopric in a large Diocese. Yet earlier, for a brief period from about 1102, the bishopric had been removed to Chester, and it is interesting to note that the name of Sir Richard de Phitun appeared as a witness to a grant of land by Robert de Masi (Massey) to the abbot of St. Werburgh's, Chester. The family was obviously keeping close to the centres of ecclesiastical power.

Their tenacity was eventually rewarded with the senior family seat established at Shawell; the junior branch settled in Cheshire when Sir Richard acquired the land of 'Falingbrome' (Fallibroome) in the parish of Wilmslow. This grant of land by the 2nd Earl of Chester, Hugh

The Fitton arms adopted from the Orreby family of Gawsworth

Cevelioc (Earl from 1135) was soon to result in the acquisition of the whole of the parish of Wilmslow for the family.

Although the family genealogy records that it was the son of the same name who took the post of justiciary of Chester in 1233, it was probably the grandson who held it for four years. This Sir Richard granted part of the Wimslow parish i.e. Fulshaw, to the Order of the Knights of St. John of Jerusalem. Sir Richard was also granted many privileges throughout Cheshire, not only for himself but also his tenants. One such concession was 'quittance from sergeant puture', this was a Forest law which enabled officers of the Crown, albeit on behalf of the Earls of Chester who represented the sovereign at that time, to claim meat and drink for themselves and attendants whilst on duty in the area it also included food for horses, hawks and hounds from anyone within the boundaries of the forest. It could be an expensive claim which Sir Richard and his tenants were spared.

At his death in 1246 Sir Richard held the manors of 'Bolyn and Falinbroome' (which had evolved from the earlier Wilmslow), the advowson of Wilmslow church and Bolyn mill etc. His son, Sir Hugh, added the manors of Rushton and Eaton to his holdings, granted by John the Scot, Earl of Chester, but these he lost together with his title, due to committing a 'felony'.

The grandson, John, remained lord of Bolyn, but it was his brother Thomas who married the widow, Isabel, daughter and heir of Thomas Orreby of Gausworth (Gawsworth); adopted the Orreby coat of arms and the spelling of Fyton when establishing his branch of the family at the Hall.

It wasn't until the reign of Richard II that Thomas's grandson gained pardon from the pious king and was knighted after royal duties in Ireland. It was this Sir Laurence who claimed the family's place in local history when the shield bearing the adopted Orreby arms was incorporated into the stonework of the Parochial Chapel (now St. Michael's) in the market place circa 1415.

Laurence outlived his son, so grandson Thomas succeeded. He took part in the Wars of the Roses and, together with '66 good Gawsworth men', fought bravely in the battle of Blore Heath near Market Drayton in 1459; for this he was knighted by Henry VI, but sadly 31 of his contin-

The present Gawsworth Hall – the Fittons came to this estate in 1316.

gent had been killed.

Once again honours skipped a generation; grandson Sir Edward was sheriff of Cheshire under Henry VIII, Treasurer of Ireland for Elizabeth I and one of the first 'modern' governors of the King Edward VI grammar school by Letters Patent 26th April 1553; he died 1579.

His son, Edward, Lord of Munster, used his influence with the queen to obtain the position of Maid of Honour for his daughter Mary in 1596. She disgraced the family by her illegitimate liaison with the Earl of Pembroke and both were sent to the Tower by Elizabeth in 1602. Her brother Edward regained favour under James I and was created baronet in 1617. Edward, however, died in August 1643 fighting at the side of Prince Rupert in support of Charles I. He was the last Fitton baronet.

Family squabbles over the inheritance of the Gawsworth estate during the next 70 years saw the demise of this staunch Roman Catholic family, when in a duel of 1712 both contenders, Lord Mohun and the Duke of Hamilton died of their wounds.

Fitton tombs and monuments in the Parish Church of St. James the Great, Gawsworth.

Wyatt Earp

The Wild West came once more to Macclesfield this week after almost a century; the previous occasion was the visit of Buffalo Bill's circus. This time it took the form of what at first glance seemed to be an inconsequential document. (N.B. this article was originally published on 4th July 2003)

I had volunteered to transcribe the text for a professor of a German university and was told only that it was in English and related to the 1880s; I therefore deduced it would relate to Victorian England.

On receipt, somewhat disappointed I found it to be an American legal document which momentarily subdued my enthusiasm, until, glancing down the second page the names of Wyatt Earp and Tombstone appeared; this was exciting. Suddenly a fascinating snippet of American history was unfolding and well worth the telling.

A certain Examiner of the Department of Justice had submitted a report to the U.S. Attorney General regarding the misconduct of a C.P. Dake, former Marshal of Arizona. The document for transcription dated March 1885 was the follow-up report accompanied by further evidence for a prosecution.

Dake, in his time as Marshal, had received over $50,000 from the Secretary of the U.S. Treasury which he had deposited as his own money, but argued that it had been used for government business although he had failed to keep any books recording transactions etc.

He claimed that between $8,000 and $12,000 dollars had been spent in suppressing the 'Cow Boy Raids, most of which he advanced to Wyatt Earp one of his deputies'. He had expected his deputies to give him receipts and vouchers for monies paid, but none had done so.

The cashier of the Bank of Arizona in Prescott, Dake's home-town, stated that the bank had never done business with Dake as a U.S. marshal, only as an individual customer, buying U.S. Treasury Warrants from him less discount; Dake deposited the money received in his own account.

Wyatt Earp wrote an informative letter confirming that a special officer of Wells Fargo & Co. had taken him to the bank in Tombstone where $2,985 had been deposited for his use. The next day Dake came to see him and confessed he had 'done something wrong . . . he had gotten drunk on wine and had drawn $340 from the deposit and spent it'. Earp's silence was requested. Earp used the remainder of the fund for 'outfitting his posse'. This was all the money he had received to quell the Cow Boy Raids and 'he never received a dollar for his service as deputy Marshal'.

Earp left the territory but Dake persuaded his bondsmen to write to him intending to bribe him for support, however Earp refused the bait. A further letter from the confidential detective of Wells Fargo & Co. revealed that Dake had contacted the General Superintending scout of the company in San Fransisco to request funds of $3,000 necessary to deal with the disturbances at Tombstone. Dake promised vouchers and results, so the money was advanced.

Dake's cronies from Prescott said that he never seemed to live as a man of money and felt he had no fortune of his own. However, the Recorder of his home county provided a list of properties purchased by both himself and his wife which neatly coincided with Dake's term of office as Marshal of Arizona (11th September 1878 – 11th July 1883).

The Examiner for the Department of Justice deduced that Dake had 'felanously converted government money entrusted to him as U.S.Marshal to his own use' and concluded 'the facts collated & presented above are of such notoriety in Tombstone, Tucson & Prescott that a perfect stranger would have no difficulty in getting track of them upon the first inquiry'

Wyatt (1848-1929), having grown up in Ilinois and Iowa alongside four brothers, then led a colourful life mostly as a lawman yet also a gambler. However he did become a church deacon of the Union Church and assistant marshall of Dodge City in 1878.

In the early 1880s Cochin County, in the extreme southeastern region of Arizona, was a lawless place. Cowboy outlaws who rustled cattle from the large ranches, regularly rode into Tombstone upsetting the elitist mine managers and their communities.

Wyatt and his brothers took up the challenge to clear the town of its notorious gangs and subdue the 'Cow Boy Raids'. As a result he, together with two of his brothers and Doc Holliday were, of course, involved in the famous gun battle near the O.K. Corral on 26th Oct. 1881. Possibly as a consequence Morgan Earp was shot and killed the following March. Wyatt shot two of the suspects and, accused of murder, fled to the boomtowns of the West. He became a legend in his own lifetime, taking part in the gold rushes and finally settling in Los Angeles. There he visited the early film studios making sure that his eventful career would not go unrecorded before dying at the good age of 80 years.

Right: An inconsequential document? No.

Opposite page: Wyatt Earp – one of the extraordinary characters of the Wild West.

Pantomimes, Books and Christmas Spirit

In the week preceding Christmas 1891 a correspondent wrote of the 'Muted Festivity' which seemed to have taken hold. Pantomimes at one or two of the large London theatres were going out of fashion, and he commented 'A something has gone out in the minds of young ladies and gentlemen who cannot read books of fairy stories' . . . This, he surmised, had contributed to taking the 'sentiment' and 'cheeriness out of Christmas', and that the 'merry dancing, singing feasting' and 'romping Christmas times' were never likely to return.

Preparing for pantomime, although they were going out of fashion by the 1890s.

perhaps there was 'comfort and sobriety within'. One has to wonder what he would have written in his column today.

But not all was doom and gloom judging from the encouragement given to playing party games, attending Christmas fairs and reading the gossip columns. Perhaps many were sitting at home engrossed in their books; certainly there was a wealth of literature promoted by the Illustrated London News with its lists of New Books and New Editions – Selected.

Lots of promotions were given space; why not buy:

'Our Christmas Number – four original stories – The Son's Veto; the Haunted Dragoon; the Inconsiderate Waiter and Their Uncle from California.'

I wonder how many were hoping to find a copy of this in their Christmas stocking.

Very much of local interest was the review given to a new edition of Mrs Gaskell's 'Cranford' (alias Knutsford as many readers will know). It was considered to have 'long taken its place amongst the standard works of fiction of the Victorian age', and would be regarded by grandchildren as a reflection of life in the mid-Victorian period, comparable to Jane Austen's novels depicting life at the end of the 18th century.

It was promoted as 'one of the most attractive gift books of the season'. Even George Sand (the assumed name of Armandine Lucile Aurore Dupin, a brilliant French novelist who had married Baron Dudevant in 1822 but was later

He concluded with a dismal picture of London on Christmas Eve; whereas once 'every fourth house glowed like a lamp, where music and merriment hummed through the casements or burst in a flood from open doors, nearly all is silence and gloom. To walk in any respectable place at midnight is like walking in a place of tombs'. He consoled himself with the thought that although there was 'dulness' everywhere,

An advertisement which covered a whole page in the Illustrated London News in December 1891.

associated with Chopin and Franz Lizt) was impressed, saying that she (Mrs. Gaskell) 'had written books which excite the deepest interest in men of the world, and yet which every girl will be better for reading'.

Although 'Cranford' was considered to have 'little that is dramatic' yet it contained 'true humour' with the reader readily able to relate to the characters; for example, Miss Jenkyns with her literary support of 'The Rambler' and her derision of 'Boz'. In part, one could sympathise with her when her prominent role in Cranford Society was taken over by Lady Glenmire and the Hon. Mrs. Jamieson.

The illustrator, Hugh Thomson, deserves much praise for his etchings, examples of which were included with the article, and to be fair, this the reviewer gave. His one small criticism was that, whilst the book depicted village life 1836-37, the men were sometimes dressed in Regency costume from a generation earlier. The females, however, so well described by Mrs. Gaskell and therefore allowing no room for poetic licence, were appropriately attired. Yet despite this, for some unknown reason, the men were more 'real' than the ladies.

For those preferring non-fiction Lord Roseberry's 'Life of Pitt', was put forward as an excellent buy, being part of a series 'Twelve English Statesmen'. On reading the columnist's evaluation of the work even this was apparently not without 'true humour'.

Apart from Lord Roseberry's personal correspondence and reflections, he called upon other contributors, one of whom was Lord Beaconsfield (Benjamin Disraeli, himself a famous novelist). Disraeli recounted that in his early days in the House of Commons Pitt's dying words had been recalled as 'Oh my country! how I leave my country!', but these were, in fact, fictitious.

One of the House of Commons waiters had told him that he had been 'called out of bed' one night when a messenger arrived in a postchaise. He was told to quickly take some of his meat pies to Pitt's house at Putney, but when the pair arrived the Statesman had already died. 'Them was his last words', the waiter declared, 'I think I will eat one of Bellamy's meat-pies!'

To all my readers, whether or not you will be taking part in a 'Big Read' or eating meat pies, do have a cheery and 'romping' good Christmas and a very Happy New Year, when they arrive.

Sir John Chandos

On the first day of January 1370 Sir John Chandos, seriously wounded, died in France. Today he might seem a somewhat remote, insignificant figure, but he is one of those fascinating characters in history who deserves notice, even if his connections with Macclesfield were for a relatively short period only.

He was descended from Richard de Chandos, a comrade of William the Conqueror. The family settled in Herefordshire along with their Coat of Arms. The junior branch subsequently moved into Derbyshire, between Ashbourne and Derby, and were also entitled to adopt the Chandos Arms together with the privileges and commitments which this entailed. The Arms appear in a glass window in the village church of Mugginton.

The year of Sir John's birth is uncertain but, as a young man by the late 1330s, he was fighting in France and Flanders on behalf of King Edward III of England. Edward was having problems with the French king Philip VI in connection with English lands in France which he claimed through his mother, Isabella. However, he had done homage to Philip for Gascony in 1329, thus accepting Philip's sovereignty. Edward obviously considered this as expedient, but Philip began to disrupt the lucrative English woollen trade with the great towns of Flanders. This was the impetus for the Hundred Years war.

In 1337 Sir John took part in the siege of Cambrai close by Valenciennes (near the French and Belgian border) in which he excelled. He was considered 'courteous, skilled and true', qualities which recommended him to Edward III as an ideal mentor and 'guardian' for his son and heir, Edward the Black Prince, and also as an important negotiator with the enemy.

By 1340 Edward III had declared himself King of France, which resulted in the great victory at Crécy in 1346 in which they all took part. There the Black Prince, only 16 years of age, won his spurs and Sir John distinguished himself, together with many others.

After their return to England the King formally instituted the Order of the Garter (c.1348-9), although it had been conceived some four years earlier. The knights numbered 26 with Sir John as a founder member; his Garter plate can still be seen above its original stall, the eleventh one on the south side of St. George's chapel, Windsor. Glimpses of his character are revealed by the famous historian Froissart.

In the summer of 1350 Edward III set sail with the English fleet to destroy that of Spain off the coast of Winchelsea. He decided to wait until the Spanish ships, laden with goods, were returning from Sluys back along the Channel to Spain. To while away the time the King, being in a jocular mood, asked the minstrels to play a dance tune which Sir John had recently brought back from Germany, and persuaded Sir John to sing along with them, much to the entertainment of the king.

A fierce sea battle ensued which the English eventually won. Afterwards they returned home and the Black Prince turned his attention to his English estates. By 1347, although only 17 years old, he made a wise decision in persuading his grandmother, Queen Isabella, to exchange the manor and forest of Macclesfield for two of his manors in Wiltshire and Dorset.

This move bears the hallmark of Sir John who would know how important the long bowmen from the Cheshire forests had been at Crécy. Problems arose however with a Macclesfield forester, Foxwist (sometimes spelt Foxtwist); his word was accepted before that of others including Robert de Legh, a riding forester of Aldelynton (Adlington), but Foxwist was soon caught out and quickly absconded.

The widowed mother of John Legh (bailiff of Macclesfield Hundred) had evidently 'taken the veil', and Legh permitted the community of nuns to work Adlington manor without permission from the Prince. He and the nuns were fined but pardoned, and when Sir John Chandos became steward of Macclesfield manor in 1353, Legh was appointed his lieutenant (deputy).

One historian suggests this was a sinecure, but Sir John was very much a 'hands on' man who would take his post seriously, and whilst in England no doubt made regular visits to the area. On 10th August 1353 he, or John Legh, was asked to provide six roe deer from the forest for a great banquet in Chester on the prince's first visit to the county. By 1356 Sir John was given desmesnes in Drakelow plus

£40 p.a. from Rudheath rents.

Sir John went on to great military successes in France, particularly at Poitiers in 1356 when he saved the Prince's life. As was customary before battle both sides sent out knights on reconnaissance and Sir John was chosen by the English. He crossed paths with a French knight who was surprised, then furious, to see Sir John wearing a lady's emblem on his arm which matched his own. Angry words were exchanged but the outcome was left to events on the battlefield; Sir John survived, the French knight did not – nothing is known of the lady.

Sir John was granted estates in Contantin, N. France, where he retired unmarried in May 1368. By December a French uprising saw Poitiers lost, and after a vain attempt to drive out the French he was pursued to the river Vienne. Many deserted but Sir John fought gallantly at the bridge of Lussac only to be badly wounded; he died the next day in Mortimer and was buried there with a superb epitaph in French placed over his grave. Even the French King grieved.

The estates were willed to Sir John's two surviving sisters and two nieces, but they never received the confiscated French possessions.

The superb brass of Sir Hugh Hastings, Norfolk, one of the founder member with Sir John Chandos of the Order of the Garter, some of whom are depicted in the borders with Edward III.

Stanley Family

Macclesfield Forest

Macclesfield forest was well superintended on behalf of the Crown, often by officials from the City of Chester, as in the instance of Sir John Chandos. These were, of course, supported by members of important local families who held, what they no doubt considered to be, prestigious positions within the hierarchy of the forest management.

Eventually the local supremo acquired the title of 'Clerk of the Manor and Forest of Macclesfield', which was held by someone well-versed in law. Over the centuries the physical forest had become very much depleted, but the administrative area remained, hence the necessity to have a clerk who made frequent visits or was well established in the area.

This meant the provision of a residence for the official from which he could operate whilst, on occasion, attending local courts held within the forest boundaries at various locations as convenient.

By the 18th century John Stafford, a prominent Macclesfield lawyer, held the post. His residence with official office was what became known as Cumberland House, a name acquired

after he had accommodated the Duke of Cumberland on his march north in pursuit of Bonnie Prince Charlie in December 1745.

On 29th January 1757 John Stafford wrote a letter to the Earl of Derby in which he confirmed that the king was Lord of the Manor of Macclesfield and formerly also of the Forest. However, he also verified that the Forest had been given as a freehold grant to the Derby family and was freehold land.

Unfortunately he gave no indication of the date of the grant, but it could have been in 1684 when, at the same time, the rents were waived from 1661; the year in which the lands had been restored to the Earls of Derby after the Civil Wars. However, there is a probability that this grant was a re-grant from an earlier period before the

Edwardian photograph of Jordangate which was originally part of Macclesfield Forest.

Civil Wars. It was made complicated by the fact that the previous Earl, and the previous King, had both been executed and many records destroyed by the Parliamentarians.

John Stafford as the Clerk was directly responsible to the Earl for the administration of forest law. The Earl's main residence was at Knowsley near Preston, so he provided local accommodation for his clerk, and circumstantial evidence suggests that over the centuries the building had always been in the area of Cumberland House, possibly on the same site. Deeds confirm that John Stafford owned the house, but do not give the name of the vendor from whom it was purchased, suggesting the land had been part of a very large estate – (? that of the Derby family).

In the 17th century the Earl still held a large portion of land from what is today the Hibel Rd. area stretching up the hill into the separate township of Hurdsfield, but this became part of the Earl's property sequestrated by the Parliamentarians.

Further circumstantial evidence suggests that in earlier centuries, after the formation of the original borough and before encroachments began, the forest boundary was on the eastern side of Mill Street, crossed the middle of what is now the Market Place opposite the parish church, and continued along the northern side of Chestergate until it met the parkland near today's Chester Rd.

When periods of turmoil took place and the kings of England were preoccupied with far greater worries, such as revolts, civil wars etc., it was an advantageous time for burgesses within boroughs to quietly extend their boundaries by the odd plot or so; even, as happened in Macclesfield, to claim town fields. But the greatest upheavals came in Cromwell's time with many legal disputes over land ownership after the Restoration.

The area of land on the opposite (i.e. eastern) side of Jordangate, now bounded by Hibel Rd., Waters Green, Jordangate and Brunswick Street, would also have been designated as forest in the early history of the borough.

By the 17th century the Swettenham family, as mentioned in previous articles, had acquired a burgage on the corner of Goose Lane (now Brunswick St.) and Jordangate, but it appears to have been in their possession much earlier. Their original holding more than likely extended down the hill towards Waters, and cov-

ered at least half the larger unit stretching to today's Hibel Rd.

But how and when could this have happened?

* * *

Influence

It is apparent that members of the Stanley family have been connected with Macclesfield Forest for centuries. One of the earliest references is in 1288, when a Roger Stanley was recorded as one of eight herditary foresters holding lands in Macclesfield Forest. His lands were at Stanley in Disley, a possible indicator of the origin of the family name. Another list of about the same time, comprising nine not eight foresters, gives the first name of Stanley as 'Grim', not Roger; perhaps this was a soubriquet, though hardly a humorous one.

By 1351 Richard Stanley held the forestership, which was included as part of the dower when his daughter married Roger Simondessone of Mottram (in-Longdendale) in 1357. It was during Richard's forestership that 'disturbances' had been taking place in the forest, resulting in the appointment of Sir John Chandos as 'master forester and and surveyor of the Cheshire forests' in 1353. This probably gave Richard the opportunity to prove himself to the 'powers that be', as Sir John was a very close companion of the young Prince Edward (the Black Prince).

Certainly the family made rapid strides during the next 50 years for, in 1403, John Stanley was appointed steward of Macclesfield forest and surveyor, chief forester and rider; he was also responsible for the forests of Delamere and Mondrem, and became steward of Prince's Henry's household (the future Henry V); the boy was16 years old. John held the office till 1412, having been granted the Isle of Man by Henry IV in 1406, by which time he was Sir John of Lathom and Knowsley, Lord of Man, Sheriff of Anglesey and Justiciar of Chester. The Stanleys at last had influence at Court.

In 1414, the year following the death of Henry IV, John Stanley was granted his forest offices for life. After his death Ralph, Lord Cromwell, took over but from 1439 the duties were shared between Cromwell and John Stanley's son, Thomas. After both had died the chief forestership remained with the Stanleys, together with the stewardship of Macclesfield Manor.

The next generation saw another Thomas

Stanley honoured, when in 1461 he became Chief Justice of Cheshire for Edward IV. This Thomas played a skilful game. Firstly in 1471 he supported his brother-in-law, the Earl of Warwick, in restoring the House of Lancaster to the throne. Ten years later he contracted a very important marriage with Margaret Beaufort, widow of Owen Tudor – and therefore mother of the exiled Henry Tudor – and secondly widow of the Duke of Buckingham.

Margaret's family was one of the wealthiest and most influential families in England. She was extremely intelligent and well educated and, with the foundation of both Christ's and St. John's colleges, one of the greatest benefactors of Cambridge University. It was also said that Sir Thomas had a superb collection of books and was very well read.

By a strange quirk of fate Sir Thomas had been embroiled in a protracted legal dispute with the Duke of Buckingham, which had begun in 1443 and lasted for three years, until Sir Thomas had failed to appear in court, realising that the Duke could afford far more legal fees than he could. The dispute was about possession of Bosley Manor, previously the property of the Macclesfield family. The Duke, of course, also owned John de Macclesfield's former 'castle' on Mill Street, which he intended to be sold upon his death together with rights to the manor. He was killed in 1460 fighting for Henry VI, but the Macclesfield sale never took place.

After the death of Edward IV, Sir Thomas was loyal to Edward V but, after the boy king's mysterious disappearance, together with his younger brother Richard, Sir Thomas quietly accepted the usurper Richard III as King.

One year after Margaret's marriage to Sir Thomas she was involved in a rebellion in support of her son, Henry. Surprisingly Thomas was granted possession of his wife's estates and made constable of England.

In June 1485 Richard III was based in Nottingham awaiting an invasion by Henry and his army of loyal supporters. Thomas Stanley excused himself and hurried home to see his family and estates, but only after sending his son, Lord Strange, to replace him, as dictated by the king. The young man was virtually a hostage, however, he gave details of a plot, which in-

Looking north to Bosley Cloud – part of Bosley Manor, once one of the wealthiest manors in England.

volved his uncle, William Stanley, and Sir John Savage, to Richard. Thomas Stanley, realising the urgency of the situation, quickly promised aid at the battle of Bosworth to the King, but the Stanley contingent arrived led by his brother William, after Thomas had supposedly succumbed to a fever. It was too late for Richard to act although he did order the death of Lord Strange; the orders were ignored and the young man escaped. William held back during the battle, thus contributing to Richard's downfall.

Sir Thomas received his title, Earl of Derby from Henry VII, but does not appear to have received the freehold of the Macclesfield forest estates until after Elizabeth I's reign.

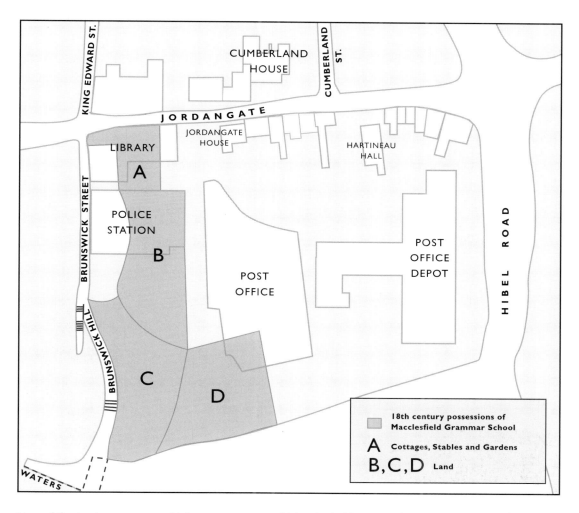

Map of the Jordangate area which was once part of Macclesfield Forest. The map also includes the areas occupied by the Macclesfield Free Grammar School in the 18th century, referred to in the following article entitled 'Jordangate'. Based on plans held by Macclesfield Borough Council and Cheshire Record Office (ref.DDX 528/7/1/1).

Jordangate

The Boundary

An area of land, stretching along both sides of King Edward Street (formerly Back Street) and continuing across Jordangate to flank Brunswick Street (formerly 'Gooselane'), has left an intriguing question to be answered. How did it become part of Macclesfield Borough by at least the 17th century?

King Edward Street in the foreground continuing across Jordangate to become Brunswick St. in the background. The stonework of the Macclesfield public library is just visible on the left behind the white car.

The area was on the northern border of the original medieval borough, wedged between the latter and the townfields, virtually cut off from the parkland and on the periphery of the forest. The 17th and 18th century property deeds which have survived lead to much conjecture.

For example, some plots with subsequent buildings erected on them, as in the instance of The Bull's Head, Market Place (originally part of Jordangate) belonged initially to the Savage family, one of whom married the daughter of Earl Rivers in 1639. By this marriage he inherited his father-in-law's title, Earl Rivers, by special Grant. Through the female line and inheritance, the Macclesfield estate passed to the Earl of Cholmondeley in the late 18th century, who,

to cover debts from his vast Nantwich estates, auctioned off the Macclesfield holdings in a grand sale which commenced in 1788.

The Savage family had leased the parkland for centuries before eventually acquiring ownership. So does this indicate that part of the Back Street area was considered parkland originally and therefore part of Macclesfield manor?

On the other hand, apart from the Savage family's overwhelming presence in Macclesfield affairs, evidenced by their chapel, effigies and grand monument in the Parish Church, there was also the Stanley family represented by the senior branch, the Earls of Derby, with their overriding authority in the surrounding forest area.

Macclesfield library viewed from the northern end. At this corner were three stables, with the gardens beginning where the white door appears on the left.

The broad strip of land in the Back Street/ Gooselane area was, therefore, ripe for encroachment by anyone who had the opportunity.

This more-than-likely came during the Wars of the Roses, particularly when Sir John Savage of Clifton married Katherine, the sister of Thomas, lst Earl of Derby, whose career was discussed in the previous article. The marriage settlement would have been an ideal opportunity to absorb this particular area, and consolidate the Savage holdings around the township, with Stanley conveniently 'turning a blind eye'.

Sir John's son, John, was created knight of the Bath by Edward IV in 1465, and elected to be coffin bearer for the king's funeral in Westminster Abbey. He was mayor of Chester 1484-85 and given many privileges by Richard III, but like Stanley he turned traitor at the Battle of Bosworth. It was his brother, however, who chose to play an important role in Macclesfield affairs.

Grammar School Properties

Thomas, having become Archbishop of York, had decided to establish a grammar school in the town and endow it with income from gifts of properties etc. This he did, with help from Sir John Percyvale, in 1504.

When Henry VIII inherited the Crown in 1509 a Macclesfield survey listed a handful of tenements on 'Jordaingate'. Whether or not at this time grammar school property was included is difficult to say. The school, originally in the Savage Chapel, was refounded in 1552 by a group of wealthy burgesses after Henry VIII's confiscation of church properties, so additional income at that time would be needed.

After the Civil Wars and Restoration the grammar school held a small strip of land along Jordangate, part of which is today represented by the pavement running alongside the new Macclesfield library. A rental list of 1667 seems to indicate that two small houses had been built on the strip, close to what is now the library entrance. They can definitely be identified on a rental list of 1731 as both having a stable, garden and croft, with the second having, in additon, a yard and building at the rear.

A third house had been added, which in size almost equalled the other two together. This house also had a stable, garden (subsequently adapted to accommodate a brewhouse as shown on a 1774 plan – see map on page 259) and croft.

Whilst the houses and stables ran south to north along Jordangate, the gardens and crofts were west to east, with the gardens immediately

The fine premises of H.T.Gaddum & Co. Ltd. 3 Jordangate and the adjacent chemist shop. On the extreme right is Cumberland House.

behind the last two stables at the northern end of the row. The crofts occupied what is now the police station car park, then spread out in a northerly direction but continued down the hill to Waters and almost to the River Bollin.

The first house was the most inconvenienced because its stable was the last one on the row; the garden was the last from Jordangate, and the croft at the bottom of the hill. The third, which had presumably become an alehouse, was fortunate; its stable was alongside, the garden was first, and its croft just past the other two small gardens at the top of the hill.

This group of tenanted grammar school properties roughly formed an L-shape, and filling up the space to form a rectangle was the burgage on which stood two houses on Gooselane belonging to Edmund Swettenham i.e. the remainder of the library site and part of the Cheshire Constabulary building.

The Swettenham Burgage

On14th August 1665 Thomas Swettenham of Birtles married Margaret, daughter of Sir Thomas Stanley of Alderley, and it appears to be from the marriage settlement that the Jordangate burgage became part of the Swettenham holdings. (Sir Thomas was descended from Sir John, brother of the 1st Earl of Derby).

The complicated situation which arose between the two branches of the Swettenham family, (see page 245) when in order to purchase Swettenham Manor back from the Davenports, Thomas acquired a loan from Edward of Somerford, effectively made Edward Swettenham owner of the Jordangate burgage. It was used as collateral together with other properties in securing the loan. Circumstantial evidence suggests that Thomas Swettenham conveyed ownership to Edward in satisfaction of part of the loan.

By 1768 the Swettenham male heirs had died out so the property passed in trust for Roger Comberbach of Chester as great-nephew. On coming of age he legally changed his name to Swettenham enabling him to inherit the estate and coat of arms. In order to redeem large land tax charges he began to sell off the Macclesfield properties including Jordangate, by then described as two dwellings in Gooselane with barns, stables, orchards etc.

On 5th April 1795 the properties passed to two trustees under a will of John Lomas, who had instructed them to invest money for the advantage of the beneficiaries. However, the actual plot of land remained with Swettenham till 1799. One of the properties passed to a victualler Isaac Oliver and became 'The Childers'. In 1818 there was a landlady in charge, Ann Oliver, but by 1825 it had become known as 'The Flying Childers', 12 Brunswick St. The landlord was Saville Smith.

The whole of the adjoining Free Grammar School property was sold to Peter Wright for £700 in 1798. Peter Wright was Macclesfield Coroner and Clerk to the Governors of the Grammar School. Related to John Stafford of Cumberland House, he appears to have taken over the Stafford legal work when John Stafford's son William died, and his office was therefore almost directly opposite this valuable area of land. He at least must have considered it valuable, for the sum he paid was considerable, particularly as at that period the Napoleonic Wars were underway.

The Pack Horse Inn

Shortly afterwards the small alehouse seems to have been enlarged on the northern side and by 1818, known as the 'Pack Horse', had Ralph Whitehouse as landlord (he appears as Whitehurst in an 1825 Directory). Rejuvenated again in 1864, an advert in the Macclesfield Courier & Herald on 28th May announced that the landlord, 'Martin Willis (late of the Sun Inn Chestergate)', thanked everyone for their kind support and confirmed that he had completed the alterations and improvements including a spacious yard and stabling.

There was a newly laid out 'Subscription' bowling green (now site of the main G.P.O. sorting office on Jordangate) which would open the following Wednesday when a 'Handsome silver snuff box given by the proprietor' would be bowled for and a dinner provided.

The demise of the inn/hotel came in the late 1960s when it stood empty for a considerable time before being demolished. The plot was eventually purchased by Cheshire County Council, together with the old District Bank on the corner (in situ since 1881 and partially on land originally used by the Pack Horse), for the building of the new library; this was officially opened on 28th April 1994 by the Duchess of Gloucester.

William Stone's House

On the opposite side of Jordangate, after the death of John Stafford of Cumberland House, in August 1775, a large house and smaller property were built on his premises and bought by a surgeon William Stone. He also owned a plot of land, stable and garden on the eastern side of the street between Pear Tree House and the Pack Horse Inn (now the wide entrance to the G.P.O. sorting office).

William Stone died in November 1815 and his widow, Ann, sold the plot, stable and garden to John Brocklehurst of Pear Tree House. The smaller property was occupied by a druggist and is a chemist shop today.

When Ann died a complicated situation arose with executors, but the large house was occupied by Thomas Grimsditch, solicitor and mayor (1833-34) who had business premises on Brunswick St. on the corner nearest the Market Place and opposite the present library. By 1863 the house was owned by the Brocklehurst family and occupied by Charles Seal 'a Music Master'. However, he was ordered 'to quit' the dwelling-house and outbuildings 3 & 5 Jordangate by Francis D. Brocklehurst on 4th September 1884. No further details are known.

Effigy in St Michael's

For many years an effigy in the southern wall of the Savage Chapel, within the Parish Church of St. Michael's, has been a subject of much speculation and debate.

The Liversage (Lyversegge) effigy in the Savage Chapel of St. Michael's Parish Church.

To begin with the figure itself is unusual and appears to be in three sections, as clearly shown by the photograph. The top third, from the waist upwards, and the bottom third, from the knees downwards, are well executed in marble. The middle portion, however, seems to be encased within a block of stone which resembles a convenient seat. The top and bottom sections are each contained within a box-like structure of stone, but with the 'lids' and one side removed so that the effigy in part can be seen.

Originally it was in the main body of the church, against the southern wall, but encased within the wall during the extensive Georgian 'modernisation' of 1740. Perhaps the figure was already concealed within its 'stone coffin' by that period, having been hidden from view, and therefore from abasement, during the religious upheavals of the mid-17th century. Certainly the beautiful Savage effigies in the neighbouring niche have suffered some vandalism. The figure, discovered during 19th century building work, was moved to its present position in the early 1880s.

The mystery regarding its entombment will probably remain, but the speculation surrounding its identity does not.

A visitor in the 17th century sketched the figure with two shields above it, one of which fitted the description of the Liversage coat of arms with its three ploughshares turned downwards, suggesting farming. From this and the description given of the coat of arms, the famous Victorian historian Earwaker correctly deduced that it did relate to a member of the Liversage family. For some reason the coat of arms was subsequently erroneously attributed to the Downes family of Pott Shrigley until my article on pages 242-243, and for some time cast doubt on the identity of the effigy.

The Lyverslegge Family

The first mention in Macclesfield of a de Lyversegge is a John in the reign of Richard II, who witnessed a burgage transfer in Wallgate during 1385. He also testified to at least four more during the following decade, proving he was a burgess; but by 1415 (during the reign of Henry V) it was a Richard de Lyversegge who took the role of witness.

This sudden appearance of the family is intriguing, for their roots can be found in the West Riding of Yorkshire around the Domesday Manor of Tateshall which, a century later, became Pontefract, one of the most important areas in Yorkshire both for wealth and noble families.

William the Conqueror's subjugation of the area saw his denizen Ilbert de Lacy build Pontefract Castle in 1086. Within this barony was Cleckheaton and Heckmondwike, and soon to be created, the township of Liversedge with its Hall, in possession of Robert de Liversedge by 1280. He became Sir Robert but had a legal battle with a relative called Thomas over a boundary dispute after Liversedge had been divided into two divisions, possibly by their father.

The family, descended from Danish stock, took as their charge on their coat of arms the symbol of a dolphin after an ancestor Dolphin de Lyversegge. They were soon into Lancashire, and a Robert appears as a witness to a charter of 1193 in Spotland (Rochdale). This branch died out with the prestigious marriage of Sir Robert's only child, Isolda, to Sir Edward Neville of Hornby Castle near Lancaster. The Nevilles then inherited the Liversedge estate.

It is probably at this time that, because of the earlier dispute, the other branch of the family at Liversedge Essolf (descended from Thomas) was forced to move into Cheshire to try to gain some of their former prestige. At the same time they took as their coat of arms the three ploughshares, this, however, was never set in stone on the Macclesfield tower of what is now St. Michael's; they were newcomers to the town.

They seem to have acquired their connections in Cheshire through the Downes or Worth families. The Downes family held the Manor of Worth through marriage during the reign Richard II in the late 14th century, and about the same time Richard de Lyversegge of Macclesfield married Thomas Worth's daughter. Her mother was Elizabeth Whelock, and because of this Richard's son, John, inherited the important Whelock estate and Hall in 1455 from his mother's brother.

In the 16th century Thomas Leversedge of Wheelock was High Sheriff of Cheshire; his sister, Douce, married Thomas Stanley of Weaver and Alderley. The Leversedge (note the spelling) coat of arms can be seen in the ceiling of the Manor of Wheelock chapel in the Parish Church of St. Mary's, Wheelock just to the south of Sandbach.

Of the Macclesfield branch, John was mayor 1440-41 and Thomas, 1468-69 and 1474-77. Thomas married into the Legh family of Adlington Hall and had a fine house in the Pearle Wall area of Jordangate, probably near to where Cumberland House now stands. It is more-than-likely his image which is depicted on the effigy in St. Michael's Parish Church.

After the battle of Flodden in 1513 many family names disappear from prominence in the history of Macclesfield, and Liversage seems to be one of them, although they continued to play an important role in the local affairs around Sandbach.

The Lyverslegge Family coat of arms.

265

Lollards

The name Lollard conjures up pictures of mysterious shadowy figures meeting in dark and remote places to perform some sort of heathen ritual. But who were they in reality, and, as myths suggest, were they connected with the Macclesfield area?

The name first surfaces about 1300 when it was given to a branch of the Cellite Order – a group of lay brothers and hospitallers who devoted themselves to providing funeral rights for the poor and caring for the sick, particularly madmen. They lived in cells – hence the name.

During the 14th century they seem to have considered themselves so virtuous that they alienated many, and Lollard was used as a derogatory term, the inference suggesting support for mad or crazy ideas. Cellites eventually united with the Servites – an order of friars and nuns 'Servants of the Blessed Mary', originally founded in 1233. In the late Victorian period there was a 'flourishing ' community of them in Fulham Rd., London.

One of the first 'outsiders' to be labelled Lollard was John Wyclif (c.1330-84) an Oxford don and philosopher. He became an employee of Henry III's government engaged in finding ways of combating papal demands which levied high taxes on the clergy. Soon, however, he went further, challenging the authority of the pope and priests and demanding that the Bible be printed in the 'Mother' tongue i.e. English for the English etc. so many could read it for themselves.

The Church stood firm believing that without guidance many would misinterpret the true meaning of the then Latin text. Later in life Wyclif oversaw the printing of the first Bible in English.

He also disclaimed the idea that during Mass the bread and wine actually became the body and blood of Christ. Further expansions of his arguments encouraged young Oxford intellectuals to rally to his support, but in 1382 (the year in which the Church engaged lay authorities to seek out the heretics) they mostly recanted or 'fled abroad'.

Wyclif inspired a certain John Huss in Bohemia also to rebel against papal dictates; his followers were known as Hussites. In 1382 Richard II married Anne of Bohemia whose father was the Holy Roman Emperor. This creates something of an enigma, because circumstantial evidence

A Staffordshire figure c. 1900 of Shakespeare's 'Falstaff', a character in Henry IV, originally named Sir John Oldcastle after a leading Lollard.

suggests that some of Anne's retinue were Hussites who joined the Lollards on arriving in England; Richard was a Dominican of the Third (lay) Order.

Saint Dominic had established his order at the personal command of the pope to quell heresy in the Church by argument and debate. The Dominicans were therefore educated to the highest level, so that they could refute heretical doctrines. This is probably why Richard tolerated the Lollards at court, hoping to win them over by argument.

Immediately after Richard's death in 1401 Henry IV ruthlessly persecuted the sect and William Sawtry was the first to be burned at the stake at Smithfield.

Many nobles who had embraced Wyclif's ideas, now conformed. The movement quietly gained momentum until risings of 1414 by Sir John Oldcastle and 1431 by a weaver, William Perkins, were quelled. Shakespeare included Oldcastle in his Henry IV but had to rename him Falstaff after a huge outcry. The sect, much diminished, did continue in a minor form until Henry VIII's reign.

Amongst the nobles was John Montagu, 3rd Earl of Salisbury, whose family had leased Bosley Manor for generations. He was one of the leading Lollards and had a Lollard priest as his chaplain. His uncle William, 2nd Earl, had held important positions under Henry III and Richard II and, as captain of Calais, had accompanied Anne of Bohemia from Gravelines, near Dunkirk, to Calais on her way to marry Richard. After William's death (1397) his widow, the dowager Countess, leased Bosley Manor to John de Macclesfield.

This Salisbury connection does suggest that Bosley could have provided a haven for Lollards but, when the persecutions began, they retreated over the neighbouring boundary into the forest of Wildboarclough. Tradition dictates that the Lollards met and worshipped there in a cave at Gradbach; however, in the reign of Henry VIII a tragedy took place.

During a service in which a 14 year old girl, Alice de Lud-auk, had, as usual, beautifully sung hymns, troops rushed in. Alice and her grandfather were killed, and the story relates that Alice was buried with respect by friends and foe alike close by the entrance of what became known as 'Lud's Church'.

The bard himself.

Ludchurch is situated in the centre of Back Forest which originally formed part of the Forest of Leek. After the Norman Conquest the forest belonged to the Earls of Chester and was granted to the Abbey of Dieulacres by Randle de Blunderville, under which jurisdiction it remained until the Dissolution of 1538; it then passed to the Crown. Henry VIII granted possession to William Trafford of Wymslow and it was at that time Alice and her grandfather were tragically killed. (for further details see *Swythamley* by Sir Philip Brocklehurst, originally a Victorian private publication but republished in 1998 by The Silk Press).

One positive fact that cannot be refuted comes from the Downes family of Pott Shrigley. When Geoffrey Downes prepared his will on 20th June 1492 he listed a Lollard or Wyclif Bible amongst his possessions. As he had organised a lending library for local worshippers, this suggests that others in the area were probably of his persuasion.

Penny Bridge

Some considerable time ago a lady wrote to me asking if I knew why the bridge over the River Bollin, adjacent to lower Hibel Road and leading to the more recent Tesco Store, was known as 'Penny Bridge'. She has lived in Hurdsfield all her life and has never been able to find the answer.

Penny Bridge over the River Bollin near Hurdsfield Rd.

I have also drawn a blank, so perhaps one or two of my readers might be able to help; however, in searching for the answer, some interesting details have emerged which, I hope, will be of interest.

The footbridge does not appear on any detailed maps before the early 1890s, but a subsequent Ordnance Survey map suggests that it was built about 1900.

A small group of friends, now retired, do recall playing in the area as young boys. The bridge was then a wooden one, but with only one bar for support, and as the young lads raced across on their bikes, one of them fell off the edge into the River Bollin. Fortunately the older boy (who wishes to remain anonymous!) rescued his friend and his bike from the water.

I have also been told by another Maxonian that some years ago, when a row of market gardens existed by the river, his donkey got out of its enclosure and, finding itself halfway across the bridge, stubbornly refused to move. Some considerable time later, after a great deal of effort and cajoling the stupified animal was finally dragged off the bridge.

The original crossing was by stepping-stones some thirty yards up stream from the bridge, and these still existed before the last war. The path, on what is now the supermarket side of the Bollin, was fenced off with a wall made of railway sleepers, because at that time the Goods yard of Hibel Road railway station occupied the area. Many of the railwaymen lived in Hurdsfield, around Nicholson Avenue etc., so for them it was a useful short cut.

A few years before the last war the wooden bridge was replaced by the metal one, which exists today, and a couple of steps were added at either end.

The path, leading in the opposite direction from the Goods yard, ran alongside the River Bollin for some distance, until it turned left and eventually joined Beech Lane just above Beech Bridge. On the opposite side of Beech Lane, but a little higher up, was the Beech Tavern, at one time a popular rendezvous, which later became a workshop for the famous cyclist Reg Harris and his bicycles.

The distance, between the footbridge and where the path turned left to Beech Lane, was occupied on the other side of the river by the Lower Hey(e)s Mill. The land on that side of the Bollin had been part of the Hurdsfield estate of the Brocklehurst family, and it was from them that the Globe Cotton Spinning and Manufacturing Company Ltd. leased the site in February 1867. The company built the original building and appropriately named it the 'Globe Mill'; it was later extended and renamed. Presumably, therefore, some of the employees, apart from those who lived in Hurdsfield, would have used the stepping stones to cross the River Bollin, as the bridge did not exist at that time.

Apart from Macclesfield's Penny Bridge, only two more come to mind. The first is in Haydock, Lancashire, a little to the east of St. Helen's on the road to Ashton-in-Makerfield. The bridge spans both the Sankey Brook and Canal. A bridge must have spanned the Brook at this point for a considerable time, because in 1755, during the reign of George II, it was proposed by Act of Parliament that the Sankey Brook be made navigable, and one of the river sections mentioned is that 'to Penny Bridge on the North branch'.

In the original proposals of the Act there was no mention made of constructing a canal, only that new cuts were permitted where considered 'proper and requisite'. In the event this loophole was used to construct a canal alongside the Sankey Brook, with double locks created just to the south of Penny Bridge. The canal made the transportation of coal from the collieries in the area a much easier task. The coal barges conveyed the coal down into the River Mersey, from where it was boated to the markets in Liverpool.

The other Penny Bridge is a village in south Cumbria, and takes its name from the bridge which, at that point, crosses the river flowing south out of Lake Coniston. In the mid-eighteenth century Charles Roe's copper ore from the Coniston mine, and destined for the smelters on Macclesfield Common, was boated down the lake to Nibthwaite. It was then carted overland to Penny Bridge or Greenodd, from where it would be taken across the notorious Morecambe Bay. Large seagoing vessels would then take the ore onboard for the journey via Liverpool and the rivers Mersey and Weaver to Northwich, where once again it would be carted overland, this time to Macclesfield.

Doves and Pigeons

This article not only concludes my 10 years of writing local history for this newspaper, but also commemorates 10 years of existence for the Macclesfield Flying Club – no, not aeroplanes but racing pigeons!

Having long been attracted to these beautiful birds, after rescuing three over the years, the last only recently, I determined to discover more about these incredible, loyal and courageous creatures.

Domestic pigeons of all varieties are descended from a common ancestor the rock dove, species Columbidae, and are more correctly called doves. However, the lovely 'white dove of peace', whilst obviously a member of the family tree, will only home within a three to four mile radius and therefore has never been used in the breeding of racing or carrier pigeons.

Man has selected and bred his winged messengers for at least 5,000 years; the earliest recorded domestication of pigeons was in Egypt (5th dynasty). Their images have appeared on mosaics, coins and figurines for centuries, the earliest found in Mesopotamia c. 4,500 B.C. Julius Caesar and Hannibal used carrier pigeons during their campaigns, subsequently followed by other historical figures such as Genghis Khan and Napoleon. By 1150 A.D. the sultan of Baghdad had established a pigeon post, and another was used to good effect during the siege of Paris 1870-71 by the General Post Office in London.

Whilst Belgium leads the world in breeding racing pigeons, Germany breeds for showing and America both for racing and producing a much larger variety as fowl for the dinner table.

British breeders take pride in their considerable contributions to the war effort during two world wars, when pigeons saved hundreds of lives. During the first, both Army and Navy set up special units and every ship, including merchantmen, had specially trained pigeons on board to return quickly with distress messages. During the last war pigeons flew on bomber and reconnaissance raids bringing back messages from ditching planes, often saving crew members brought down over the sea. Many flew through terrible conditions, snow blizzards and storms, some badly injured such as one which had been hit in the eye with an enemy bullet. And a handful just managed their loft to drop down dead from exhaustion, but with the message safely delivered; in all 31 pigeons were awarded the Dicken medal for their outstanding performances.

Altogether 200,000 pigeons were given by breeders to the war effort, each worth from £2 to £5. The largest sum ever paid for a pigeon £125,000, a Belgium Jan-Aarden bird, was in 1994 by a famous Italian descendant in

Above: Beehive, Black Rd., rendezvous of the Macclesfield pigeon fanciers; inset – a racing pigeon.

Above: one of the beautiful doves which frequent South Park.

Right: Adlington Hall, the Elizabethan East Wing – to the rear and right stood an impressive three-storey dovehouse in the 18th century;

Leicester, Louis Masserella, ice cream entrepreneur and breeder, not only of pigeons, but also famous race horses, amongst them, of course, Mr. Softie.

Many pigeons are listed on a meritorious list, including Royal Blue, owned and trained by King George VI from the Royal Lofts at Sandringham. It was the first pigeon in the last war (October 1940) to bring back a message which was from a stranded aircrew in Holland.

Much further afield a Macclesfield pigeon fancier, Frank Hough, was also making his contribution. He was in the Army Pigeon Service, firstly in Burma and India, and eventually set up units in territory infiltrated by the Japanese. He worked alongside Gurkhas and had to deal with jungle conditions, including birds of prey, and local tribesmen.

* * *

Originally there were four Pigeon Fanciers Clubs in Macclesfield, three of which amalgamated in 1994 to become The Macclesfield Flying Club, which now meets at the Beehive on Black Road.

Macclesfield & District, formed 1910-20, was the first; it met at the King's Head, Chestergate before moving to the Commercial (now the Boar Hound) Brook St., then to the Bruce Arms, Crompton Rd. where it changed its name to the Broken Cross Flying Club and subsequently moved to the Broken Cross Institute until 1994.

Macclesfield Central was started c. 1939 by Albert Broomhead of Hurdsfield Rd. It first met

in the Royal Oak, Pickford St., but after several moves, including the Dolphin, Windmill St.; the Nag's Head, Waters Green and the Red Lion (now the Barnfield) Catherine St., it moved to the Beehive on amalgamation.

Macclesfield Premier, founded in the 1940s, was happy to remain with 'the Swan' (White Swan), Rodney St., until it too moved to the Beehive. It left behind a mid-week club, The Three Birds, which, although still registered, is inactive at present.

Macclesfield Flying Club is now part of the Staffordshire & Moorlands District Federation. It joined East Cheshire in 1994 (originally the individual clubs had been with Stockport), but due to disbandment was forced to change allegiance.

* * *

Adlington Hall is the venue for an entertaining story relating to a dove, but referred to as a pigeon by Elizabeth Legh (1694-1734). She was an exceptional harpsichord player and a great admirer of Handel. When home from London, at her father's Hall, she played in the room nearest to the impressive three-storey dovehouse. Whenever she played 'Spera si in Otho', an air by Handel, the bird would fly from the dovehouse and alight on the window sill, giving signs of enjoying the performance. There it remained until the final note when it flew back again. As it never appeared for any other piece, Elizabeth renamed the composition the 'Pigeon Air'.

Whalley Hayes

Whilst the Whalley Hayes car park site is featuring in the headlines at present because of a proposed redevelopment, I am taking the opportunity to feature it because of its interesting historic past.

The present Whalley Hayes car park site.

Situated a little to the north-west of the ancient medieval borough, surprisingly the land was in private ownership from at least the 17th century, possibly earlier. As its early history is somewhat obscure, it is important to compare it with the surrounding area, and see if it fits into a pattern.

* * *

In 1748 the then Free Grammar School (now The King's School), moved into new premises on Back Street (today King Edward Street) which included a large area of land. The present school is sited on, and still retains, a little more than a quarter of that original area.

The land, totalling just over 30 statute acres (not Cheshire acres which were more than twice the size), was made up of six parts, the largest was the Great Whalley heys; the old Infirmary, together with its grounds, and West Park subsequently occupied this area. The grammar school holdings continued into the Middle Field and Putt hills, the latter now taken up by the Cemetery.

The Little Whalley heys of just over two statute acres, is still retained by The King's School as part of its lower playing field adjacent to the Bollinbrook estate. But whether or not the site of the Whalley Hays car park was originally part of the Great Whalley heys, is unclear, it seems to have been given the name for convenience as its northern boundary is defined by the lane called Whalley Hayes.

It has been suggested that the hayes, heys or

eyes were medieval enclosures for animals, but so far I have been unable to confirm this. They appear to have been enclosed for the use of the burgesses and more than likely for the purpose of growing crops, although one or two were possibly used as pasture. There is no specific mention of the name or names in any of the early records, and the deriviation has so far eluded me except an old alternative – hay i.e. referring to the crop.

They are certainly mentioned in the 17th century and had apparently been acquired by the burgesses at some convenient time in the past as an encroachment.

* * *

Apart from the Great Whalley and Little Whalley heys, there was the Horsehey (which seems to have been near the river Bollin in Lower Hurdsfield); the Lower Eyes (around what is now the Sunderland Street which later became Pickford Eyes), and the adjoining Sutton Eyes along the banks of the Bollin in the Mill Lane area.

It is interesting to note that, apart from the Great Whalley heys, they were all situated along the banks of the Bollin and formed an arc to the north and east of the town.

(There is, of course, reference to Parkett Heyes in the name of the road at Broken Cross. This is the odd one out and as yet something of a mystery).

The remainder of the encirclement was completed by the Lord's park to the south and west. And whilst the parkland area has been subjected to the force of the weather over the centuries, particularly as the wind sweeps across the Cheshire Plain, yet the area of the enclosures has been more sheltered under the hills of the town.

The burgesses, if challenged about the encroachments, would no doubt argue that much of the land had been boggy or marshy and therefore unadopted, and they had drained and cultivated it with time and effort. Certainly the Pickford family was claiming this in the mid-17th century.

* * *

The only circumstantial evidence for the Great Whalley heys having been part of the parkland is that by the time the grammar school took it over, a strip of land on either side was owned by General Cholmondeley, the owner of the parkland. There seems no necessity for him to have purchased these plots, and they seem to have been gained by inheritance.

The Townfield stretched from Chester Road, (with the portion called the Gallowfield adjacent to the main road for obvious reasons!), across the area now occupied by the West Park Hospital and the area formerly occupied by Parkside Hopital, then continued across Victora Road until it reached Broken Cross. This was the original Rowode (Roewood) cleared of its trees and claimed by the burgesses for their use, which came under dispute with the Crown on occasion.

The lower part of Chestergate was therefore an area ripe for encroachment by the burgesses, particularly during traumatic periods of English history when the Crown was 'otherwise engaged'.

Having become privately owned the greater part of the car park site seems to have remained as crofts or gardens until well into the 18th century. But by the late 17th century development began on its southern boundary bordering Back Street.

There was a right of way which started about halfway along the plot and led from Back Street for a few feet, then turned left to exit on what is now Grosvenor Street. It had the unusual name of Blindman's Lane, and was presumably for convenient access to some of the crofts or gardens. At this time these small enclosures appear to have been used as market gardens, however, with the arrival of the silk button industry during the mid-17th century, the area, in fact Macclesfield in general, was about to begin a new era.

Development

It was not until the beginning of the 20th century that the whole of the Whalley Heyes car park site began to be developed as one unit. From medieval times it had been in several occupations, and later under several ownerships, creating a somewhat complicated situation from the historical point of view.

However, sufficient information and deeds have survived to allow for an overall clearer picture of its development, and for convenience it can be divided into four parts.
1) The western third of the area, which is now partly bordered by Grosvenor Street on the west, and the beginning of Prestbury Road (odd number 1-11) on the south, was not developed until after 1800 and was part of Orme's Croft.

It had remained leased as individual plots, which in all probability were mostly market gardens, although one or two seem to have been ornamental gardens.

2) This also applied to a narrower strip of land which ran along the whole of the northern boundary, and today lies contiguous with the right of way called Whalley Hayes.

3) Another, though very small plot, comprising the corner of King Edward Street and Westminster Road, was, by the 19th century, occupied by four houses with addresses on King Edward Street. On 6th February 1884 the plot and houses were bought by Macclesfield Corporation from a Samuel Downes to be utilised as a service station site.

4) The remainder of the site i.e. the middle section with its slightly curving south-west boundary running along King Edward Street, is the most interesting and the one to be developed first. As previously mentioned, the earlier street name was Back Street, with Blindman's Lane a convenient short cut to Prestbury Lane.

At that time Grosvenor Street was non-existent; in fact it does not appear on any deed until 1st August 1889 when the proposal to lay it out was included. It was to be 5ft wide, and taken out of a plot of land which had been 'acquired' by a Thomas Leadbetter; he therefore became responsible for the 'flagged footway or path' which had to be created. As this passed through his land he had the unenviable task of repairing it from time to time as necessary.

The story of the middle section (no.4) can now be told.

Silk

By the 1740s, probably earlier, the Swindells family owned the whole of this part which was leased out to individuals. It passed down through the family (first a John, then a Humphrey) until it was inherited by two brothers, John and David Swindells. At that time it was a piece of meadow land or pasture, with a barn possibly already on the land. As John Swindells was a joiner and architect, it seems to have encouraged the pair to develop the area as an investment by building on it.

On 31st July 1773 the brothers leased to a John Garrett, gentleman of Newcastle-under-Lyme, five houses all tenanted; a garden and a parcel of enclosed meadow land which had previously been a croft. On part of the meadow was the barn and 3 or 4 bays of buildings, the latter occupied by a silk partnership of Jonas Hall and Philip Clowes. The interesting fact is that the premises of Hall and Clowes occupied the site of a former twisting croft.

It seems more than likely that it was Hall & Clowes who had first created the twisting croft and then converted it into a more sizeable business. Jonas is shown on the 1756 Land Tax return as leasing two houses with gardens and three workshops from Joseph Jackson on Chestergate, and also as a partner of Thomas Bunnell on Barn St. (now part of Churchill Way) where they owned their own workshop.

A twisting croft was about 25 yards long and 5 yards wide, originally created in the 17th century for the primitive twisting of silk threads before the advent of machines, (each of the latter was initially known as a mill). The twisting was done with two twisters; often young boys worked with older women. Several threads were stretched out along the length of the croft from bobbins on a belt usually around a child's or young person's waist; these were then twisted together to form a single thread and wound onto a contraption resembling a penny farthing bicycle, but with the large wheel over the smaller one. The process was repeated several times until a substantial thread was produced which was then wound into hanks (see the French illustration) ready for dyeing.

On the opposite or southern side of Back St. was an area of land bought by Josiah Smale on 17th Aug. 1761, on which he had also begun development. In June 1771, in order to provide his daughter with money (probably her dowry) he was able to sell a house with appurtenances and an adjoining twisting croft described as a parcel of land on which stood a twisting shade (shed). Josiah Smale, a twister (of the silk variety!), was paid £280 by Benjamin Mather, a Macclesfield chapman, for the premises.

There is also evidence in other property deeds of twisting crofts behind properties on both sides of lower Jordangate in the 18th century, and no doubt more await discovery.

* * *

The next stage in the development of the car park site returns once more to the two Swindells brothers.

In May 1775 John and David Swindells released a plot of land and some of their properties to a Samuel Boyce, and only four months later, in September 1775, John sold David his

This illustration is from Diderot's Encyclopedie (1751-77) showing the various methods used in France for winding the twisted silk into hanks ready for dyeing.

half of the plot for £100. In order to make the purchase David Swindells borrowed the money from Boyce. Two years later (September 1777) Boyce lent Swindells a further £100, and in return the ownership of the plot was transferred to him.

The Swindells brothers retained a garden for their own use and continued leasing out the remainder of their land and properties viz: the five houses near Back St. together with the barn and building. Philip Clowes seems to have left the partnership and Jonas Hall is shown as sole lessee in May 1775. By then there were eight houses, three workshops and three gardens; two years later another house had been built.

All these buildings were leased to individuals but were quickly bought and sold by a speculator, Thomas Ward in November and December 1784. The purchaser was Joseph Roe, son of the deceased industrialist Charles, who must have

considered the purchase as a good investment. Three years later, with the establishment of the Hawkins & Mills bank on Jordangate, he sold it to one of the Roe & Co. partners, Robert Hodgson of Congleton, who had a loan from the bank. By then the buildings are recorded as a 'Shade {shade} or Factory, Singeing house {essential to the silk twisting process}, Cart house, Stables', and other buildings which in part were occupied by two twisters and two dyers.

This property passed through several hands and is recorded in 1833 as owned by a Thomas Stayley who, on 2nd September that year, sold the 'parcel of land . . . near a certain Street there formerly called Back Street but now called King Edward Street' and adjacent to Blindman's Lane and a yard called Hay's Yard, together with the silk factory and other buildings, to a family group, surname Woodward, and a John Holland, partners and silk manufacturers.

By this time the nine houses were still included, but appear to have been designated numbers 4 to 12 of Court 11. Originally six of them fronted the street when built, but shortly afterwards a row of 12 houses was completed in front of them, along the very edge of the street.

Orme's Croft

This relates to part 1) of the area i.e. the land bordered by Grosvenor St. on the west, Prestbury Road on the south and continuing part way along King Edward St. This was part of Orme's Croft in possession of Thomas Mather of Legh Hall, who had inherited the fairly substantial plot. On 15th November 1804 he decided to allow development to begin and firstly let a small plot fronting what is now King Edward St. to Charles Deane a cabinet maker. The deeds stipulate that within one year Deane had to build one or more houses or buildings:

'in a good substantial and workmanlike manner with brick or stone or both to be set in lime Mortar and the floors and roof timbers to be of good sound Oak or fir timber and covered with Slates or flags . . .'.

They also had to be two storeys high and if the tenants needed repairs carrying out these had to be done within one month. This is typical of many Georgian property deeds of the period.

This plot was virtually surrounded by land which had been acquired by an engineer, David Hays from the Swindells' inheritance.

Iron Foundry

Another part of Orme's Croft was sold by Mather to an ironmonger, Robert Greaves, on 14th December 1814. This was much bigger than Deane's plot and occupied what is now the corner of Prestbury Road and King Edward St. During 1815 (when Napoleon was finally defeated) Greaves erected an iron foundry on the site, but by 1818 had been declared bankrupt. By that time he was described as a publican but also 'a Prisoner in the Gaol of Chester Castle'.

This iron foundry was converted by a relative, Charles Greaves, into a silk factory with an engine house and outbuildings, and then into two silk factories. This was, in due course, also sold to the Woodward and Holland partnership trading as 'Messrs. Woodward & Co. Eventually what became a whole silk mill complex was sold to Thomas Johnson in 1895.

Hay's Yard

The remainder of the Swindells holdings had passed to trustees and eventually on 1st September 1815 one of them, Charles Lowe a farmer of Brereton, let his share of the land to David Hays. Hays was an engineer who intended building ten houses. In the event six were built on the southern side of what was called Hay's Yard, and three on the northern side. Access was through a passage way from King Edward St. and the yard was situated behind the plot sold by Thomas Mather to Charles Deane on 15th November 1804.

Royal George Row

The story, in relation to the plot of land transferred to Samuel Boyce by David Swindells, can now be told. This was the land bordering the eastern side of Thomas Mather's inheritance of Orme's Croft and the land leased to David Hays part of which became Hay's Yard (see plan).

On 1st January 1779 Boyce sold to Richard Allen, a silk twister, that part of the plot originally occupied by the twisting croft and was then converted back to a garden by Allen. He also demolished the few small buildings on site and erected a building near to Blindman's Lane, presumably connected with silk production, but retained a small piece of land on the northern side.

Richard Allen, having completed his development sold the building and a small area of adjoining land to Samuel Bower, a gentleman of Newcastle-under-Lyme, who must have bought it as an investment for leasing out. The remainder of the plot, which was contiguous with what was then Back St. Allen, sold to John Lowe a peruke maker, and Thomas Burgess a chapman, both of Macclesfield.

By 1782 Burgess and Lowe had built the 12 cottages along Back St. which were given the name the 'Royal George Row'. These subsequently became numbers 73-95 King Edward St. and would survive until after the Second World War, by which time the cottages in Court 11 had been demolished.

The story of how the row was given its name is an interesting but tragic one. The Royal George was the flagship of Admiral Richard Kempenfelt. He had had a decisive victory over the French fleet, although facing a much superior force, whilst on duty in the Channel during December 1781. He had served the navy well during his long career and had provided a better

The corner of King Edward St. and Prestbury Rd. The area on the left was where an 18th Century iron foundry was originally built. (See plan on pages 280-281).

King Edward St. The Royal George Row was sited on the left-hand side between the two electric light columns. The mill building on the right was connected to the Royal George Mill on the left by an overhead covered walkway.

code of signals; he was well respected and a bold adversary.

On 29th August 1782 he sailed into Spithead to enabled the Royal George to receive 'a parliamentary heel' i.e. instead of being in dry dock so that she could be cleaned below the water line, it meant that she was weighed down on one side whilst at anchorage so that the other side was raised above the water line to allow for cleaning and any necessary repairs.

Most of the officers and hundreds of seamen were on board, together with many wives and children who were visiting. Surprisingly everyone was allowed to remain on the ship whilst she was being fitted for sea. The terrible tragedy then occurred, she sank with everyone on board, Kempenfelt included, and all were drowned.

The Admiralty accepted the explanation that water had run in at the portholes, but the navy thought differently, considering that she had been under severe strain and that a piece of rotten timber had fallen out. She had been built in 1756 and was known to have been 'notoriously rotten' for sometime.

The Admiralty insisted that she should not be raised, causing further speculation that the truth was not to be revealed. Such was the tragedy that the nation mourned. Amazingly my 97 year old father recalls that, when he was a young boy at school just before the I World War, the children were taught a song about the sinking of the Royal George; this he has sung to me. It seems incredible that 130 years after the event those children were still being taught to remember the dreadful disaster.

We were fortunate to find the poem, 'Loss of the Royal George', written by William Cowper (1831-80) which had inspired the shorter version put to music and is reproduced on the opposite page.

The Royal George Row remained until the 1950s when the properties and land together with what remained of Court 11 were bought by a company called Neckwear Ltd.

This company, whose registered office became Grosvenor St. Macclesfield were of Arkwright House, Manchester. Surprisingly the company had first made its appearance on the site in 1911, and slowly but surely over the years bought up all the other plots of land and buildings, eventually owning the whole site. Despite the name the company made ladies' tops and dresses, and embroidery was also an important part of the work.

On 31st December 1964 Neckwear Ltd. sold out to a firm called Conlowe, who in turn sold to English Sewing Ltd. on 10th November 1966. In May 1968 English Sewing Ltd. became English Calico Ltd. The firm sold to a speculator, Dean Smith, via agents in March 1972, and it was Smith who negotiated with Macclesfield Borough Council to finalise the sale of the whole site in November 1975.

By 1976 the site had been completely cleared of all buildings and converted into the present Whalley Hayes Car Park. Fortunately a plan, circa mid-20th century, has survived showing that there was an overhead walkway above King Edward St. linking the rear of a mill on Chestergate with the Grosvenor St. and Royal George Mills, as they were called; all in possession of Neckwear Ltd.

Loss of the Royal George

Toll for the brave-
The brave that are no more!
All sunk beneath the wave
Fast by their native shore!

Eight hundred of the brave,
Whose courage well was tried,
Had made the vessel heel
And laid her on her side.

A land-breeze shook the shrouds
And she was overset;
Down went the Royal George,
With all her crew complete.

Toll for the brave!
Brave Kempenfelt is gone;
His last sea-fight is fought
His work of glory done.

It was not in the battle;
No tempest gave the shock;
She sprang no fatal leak,
She ran upon no rock.

His sword was in its sheath,
His fingers held the pen,
When Kempenfelt went down
With twice four hundred men.

Weigh the vessel up
Once dreaded by our foes!
And mingle with our cup
The tears that England owes.

Her timbers yet are sound,
And she may float again
Full charged with England's thunder,
And plow the distant main;

But Kempenfelt is gone,
His victories are o'er;
And he and his eight hundred
Shall plow the wave no more.

William Cowper (1731-1800).

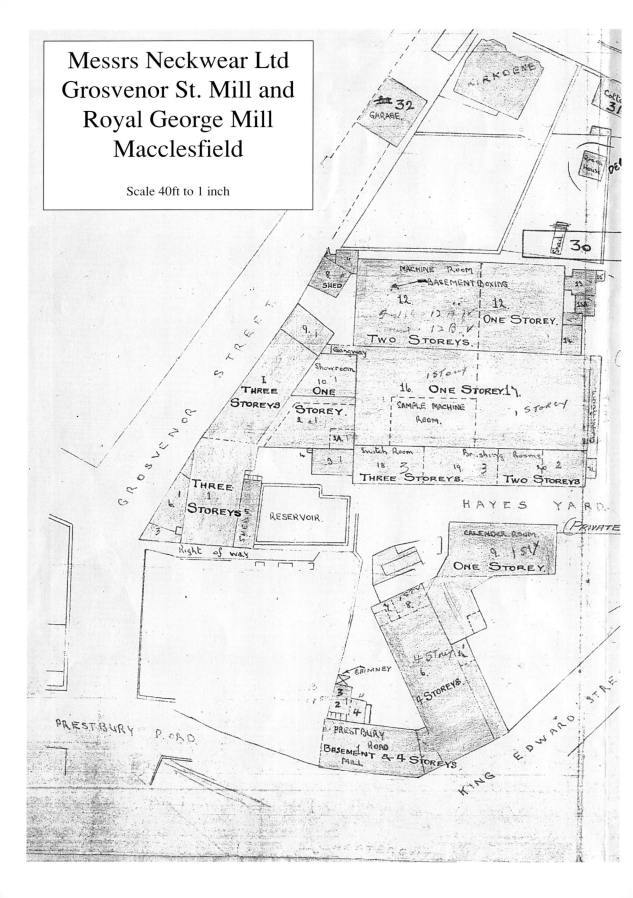

Messrs Neckwear Ltd Grosvenor St. Mill and Royal George Mill Macclesfield

Scale 40ft to 1 inch

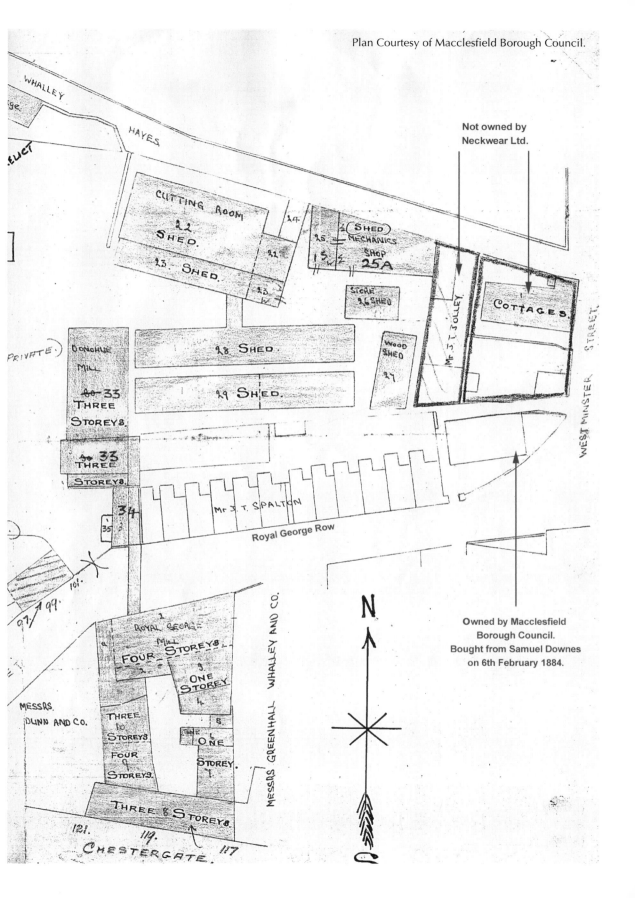

Plan Courtesy of Macclesfield Borough Council.

Not owned by
Neckwear Ltd.

WHALLEY

HAYES

CUTTING ROOM
22
SHED.
24
23. SHED.
32
23
W

SHED
MECHANICS
SHOP
25A
25
S
W

STORE
26 SHED

(PRIVATE.)

DONOHUE
MILL
to 33
THREE
STOREYS.

28 SHED.

29 SHED.

WOOD
SHED
27

Mr J.T.JOLLEY.

COTTAGES.

WEST MINSTER STREET.

to 33
THREE
STOREYS.

34

35

Mr J.T. SPALTON

Royal George Row

101

97, 99

ROYAL GEORGE
MILL
FOUR STOREYS.
2
ONE
STOREY
4
3
5

MESSRS.
DUNN AND CO.

THREE
to
STOREYS
FOUR
STOREYS.

ONE
STOREY.

MESSRS. GREENHALL WHALLEY AND CO.

THREE & STOREYS.

121   119.
CHESTERGATE.   117

N

Owned by Macclesfield
Borough Council.
Bought from Samuel Downes
on 6th February 1884.

A Note on References

Most of the information has been gleaned from property deeds often in possession of owners or their representatives, but for the vast majority I do hold relevant photocopies. The remainder has been obtained from The Dictionary of National Biography; The Oxford English Dictionary; J.P. Earwaker's *East Cheshire* (1880); G. Ormerod's *History of Cheshire* (2 Edn.1882); *Britannica Micropaedia* and Local Studies in libraries relevant to the area of my researches, including, of course, the local collections in the Macclesfield Public Library and the Cheshire Record Office.

Index

Vol. I (pages 1-144) & Vol. II (pages 145-288)